YOUTH JUSTICE

FOCUS ON SOCIAL WORK LAW
Series Editor: Alison Brammer

Palgrave Macmillan's Focus on Social Work Law series consists of compact, accessible guides to the principles, structures and processes of particular areas of the law as they apply to social work practice. Designed to develop students' understanding as well as refresh practitioners' knowledge, each book provides focused, digestible and navigable content in an easily portable form.

Available now

Looked After Children, Caroline Ball
Safeguarding Adults, Alison Brammer
Court and Legal Skills, Penny Cooper
Child Protection, Kim Holt
Capacity and Autonomy, Robert Johns
Making Good Decisions, Michael Preston-Shoot
Children in Need of Support, Joanne Westwood

Forthcoming titles

Mental Health, Christine Hutchison and Neil Hickman
Adoption and Permanency, Philip Musson

Author of the bestselling textbook *Social Work Law*, Alison Brammer is a qualified solicitor with specialist experience working in Social Services, including child protection, adoption, mental health and community care. Alison coordinates the MA in Child Care Law and Practice and the MA in Adult Safeguarding at Keele University.

Series Standing Order

ISBN 9781137017833 paperback
(*outside North America only*)

You can receive future titles in this series as they are published by placing a standing order. Please contact your bookseller or, in the case of difficulty, write to us at the address below with your name and address, the title of the series and the ISBN quoted above.

Customer Services Department, Macmillan Distribution Ltd
Houndmills, Basingstoke, Hampshire RG21 6XS, England

YOUTH JUSTICE

JO STAINES

First published 2015 by
PALGRAVE

Palgrave in the UK is an imprint of Macmillan Publishers Limited, registered
in England, company number 785998, of 4 Crinan Street, London N1 9XW.

Palgrave Macmillan in the US is a division of St Martin's Press LLC,
175 Fifth Avenue, New York, NY 10010.

Palgrave is a global imprint of the above companies and is represented
throughout the world.

Palgrave® and Macmillan® are registered trademarks in the United States,
the United Kingdom, Europe and other countries

ISBN: 978–1–137–33934–8

This book is printed on paper suitable for recycling and made from fully
managed and sustained forest sources. Logging, pulping and manufacturing
processes are expected to conform to the environmental regulations of the
country of origin.

A catalogue record for this book is available from the British Library.

A catalog record for this book is available from the Library of Congress.

Typeset by Cambrian Typesetters, Camberley, Surrey

Printed in China

CONTENTS

TABLE OF CASES

TABLE OF LEGISLATION

ACKNOWLEDGMENTS

My thanks go to Palgrave Macmillan for allowing me the opportunity to write this book and to the students in the School for Policy Studies, University of Bristol, for inspiring me to do so. I am indebted to my family and friends for their support, patience and encouragement without which this book could not have been written.

Contains public sector information licensed under the Open Government Licence v3.0.

ABBREVIATIONS

ABCs	acceptable behaviour contracts
ADHD	attention deficit hyperactivity disorder
ASBA 2003	Anti-Social Behaviour Act 2003
ASBO	anti-social behaviour order
BME	black and minority ethnic
CBO	criminal behaviour order
CDA 1998	Crime and Disorder Act 1998
CJA 2003	Criminal Justice Act 2003
CJIA 2008	Criminal Justice and Immigration Act 2008
CJPOA 1994	Criminal Justice and Public Order Act 1994
CPS	Crown Prosecution Service
CRAE	Children's Rights Alliance for England
CYPA 1933	Children and Young Persons Act 1933
DCSF	Department for Children, Schools and Families
DTO	detention and training order
ECHR	European Convention on Human Rights 1953
EDS	extended determinate sentence
EPP	extended sentences for public protection
HM	Her Majesty's
IF	intensive fostering
IPNA	injunctions to prevent nuisance and annoyance
IPP	imprisonment for public protection
IQ	intelligence quotient
ISS	intensive supervision and surveillance
LASCH	local authority secure children's home
LASPO 2012	Legal Aid, Sentencing and Punishment of Offenders Act 2012
LSCB	Local Safeguarding Children Board
MACR	minimum age of criminal responsibility
MAPPA	Multi-Agency Public Protection Arrangements

MCA 1980	Magistrates' Courts Act 1980
MHA 1983	Mental Health Act 1983
MoJ	Ministry of Justice
NOMS	National Offender Management Service
OBTJ	offences brought to justice
PACE 1984	Police and Criminal Evidence Act 1984
PCC(S)A 2000	Powers of the Criminal Courts (Sentencing) Act 2000
PCSO	police and community support officer
PSR	pre-sentence report
RPI	restrictive physical intervention
SAF	Single Assessment Framework
SGC	Sentencing Guidelines Council
SOCPA 2005	Serious Organised Crime and Police Act 2005
SSP	Safer Schools Partnership
SSR	sentence specific report
STC	secure training centre
UN	United Nations
UNCRC	United Nations Convention on the Rights of the Child 1989
UNICEF	United Nations Children's Fund
YCC	youth conditional caution
YIP	Youth Inclusion Programme
YISP	Youth Inclusion and Support Panel
YJB	Youth Justice Board for England and Wales
YJCE 1999	Youth Justice and Criminal Evidence Act 1999
YOI	young offender institution
YOP	Youth Offender Panel
YOT	Youth Offending Team
YRD	youth restorative disposal
YRO	youth rehabilitation order

USING THIS BOOK

Aim of the series

Welcome to the Focus on Social Work Law Series.

This introductory section aims to elucidate the aims and philosophy of the series; introduce some key themes that run through the series; outline the key features within each volume; and offer a brief legal skills guide to complement use of the series.

The Social Work Law Focus Series provides a distinct range of specialist resources for students and practitioners. Each volume provides an accessible and practical discussion of the law applicable to a particular area of practice. The length of each volume ensures that whilst portable and focused there is nevertheless a depth of coverage of each topic beyond that typically contained in comprehensive textbooks addressing all aspects of social work law and practice.

Each volume includes the relevant principles, structures and processes of the law (with case law integrated into the text) and highlights clearly the application of the law to practice. A key objective for each text is to identify the policy context of each area of practice and the factors that have shaped the law into its current presentation. As law is constantly developing and evolving, where known, likely future reform of the law is identified. Each book takes a critical approach, noting inconsistencies, omissions and other challenges faced by those charged with its implementation.

The significance of the Human Rights Act 1998 to social work practice is a common theme in each text and implications of the Act for practice in the particular area are identified with inclusion of relevant case law.

The series focuses on the law in England and Wales. Some references may be made to comparable aspects of law in Scotland and Northern Ireland, particularly to highlight differences in approach. With devolution in Scotland and the expanding role of the Welsh Assembly Government it will be important for practitioners in those areas and working at the borders to be familiar with any such differences.

Features

At a glance content lists

Each chapter begins with a bullet point list summarizing the key points within the topic included in that chapter. From this list the reader can see 'at a glance' how the materials are organized and what to expect in that section. The introductory chapter provides an overview of the book, outlining coverage in each chapter that enables the reader to see how the topic develops throughout the text. The boundaries of the discussion are set including, where relevant, explicit recognition of areas that are excluded from the text.

Key case analysis

One of the key aims of the series is to emphasize an integrated understanding of law, comprising legislation and case law and practice. For this reason each chapter includes at least one key case analysis feature focusing on a particularly significant case. The facts of the case are outlined in brief followed by analysis of the implications of the decision for social work practice in a short commentary. Given the significance of the selected cases, readers are encouraged to follow up references and read the case in full together with any published commentaries.

On-the-spot questions

These questions are designed to consolidate learning and prompt reflection on the material considered. These questions may be used as a basis for discussion with colleagues or fellow students and may also prompt consideration or further investigation of how the law is applied within a particular setting or authority, for example, looking at information provided to service users on a council website. Questions may also follow key cases, discussion of research findings or practice scenarios, focusing on the issues raised and application of the relevant law to practice.

Practice focus

Each volume incorporates practice-focused case scenarios to demonstrate how the law is applied to social work practice. The scenarios may be fictional or based on an actual decision.

Further reading

Each chapter closes with suggestions for further reading to develop knowledge and critical understanding. Annotated to explain the reasons for inclusion, the reader may be directed to classic influential pieces, such as enquiry reports, up-to-date research and analysis of issues discussed in the chapter, and relevant policy documents. In addition students may wish to read in full the case law included throughout the text and to follow up references integrated into discussion of each topic.

Websites

As further important sources of information, websites are also included in the text with links from the companion website. Some may be a gateway to access significant documents including government publications, others may provide accessible information for service users or present a particular perspective on an area, such as the voices of experts by experience. Given the rapid development of law and practice across the range of topics covered in the series, reference to relevant websites can be a useful way to keep pace with actual and anticipated changes.

Glossary

Each text includes a subject-specific glossary of key terms for quick reference and clarification. A flashcard version of the glossary is available on the companion website.

Visual aids

As appropriate, visual aids are included where information may be presented accessibly as a table, graph or flow chart. This approach is particularly helpful for the presentation of some complex areas of law and to demonstrate structured decision-making or options available.

Companion site

The series-wide companion site www.palgrave.com/socialworklaw provides additional learning resources, including flashcard glossaries, web links, a legal skills guide, and a blog to communicate important developments and updates. The site will also host a student feedback zone.

Key sources of law

In this section an outline of the key sources of law considered through-out the series is provided. The following 'Legal skills' section includes some guidance on the easiest ways to access and understand these sources.

Legislation

The term legislation is used interchangeably with Acts of Parliament and statutes to refer to primary sources of law.

All primary legislation is produced through the parliamentary process, beginning its passage as a Bill. Bills may have their origins as an expressed policy in a government manifesto, in the work of the Law Commission, or following and responding to a significant event such as a child death or the work of a government department such as the Home Office.

Each Bill is considered by both the House of Lords and House of Commons, debated and scrutinized through various committee stages before becoming an Act on receipt of royal assent.

Legislation has a title and year, for example, the Equality Act 2010. Legislation can vary in length from an Act with just one section to others with over a hundred. Lengthy Acts are usually divided into headed 'Parts' (like chapters) containing sections, subsections and paragraphs. For example, s. 31 of the Children Act 1989 is in Part IV entitled 'Care and Supervision' and outlines the criteria for care order applications. Beyond the main body of the Act the legislation may also include 'Schedules' following the main provisions. Schedules have the same force of law as the rest of the Act but are typically used to cover detail such as a list of legislation which has been amended or revoked by the current Act or detailed matters linked to a specific provision, for instance, Schedule 2 of the Children Act 1989 details specific services (e.g. day centres) which may be provided under the duty to safeguard and promote the welfare of children in need, contained in s. 17.

Remember also that statutes often contain sections dealing with inter-pretation or definitions and, although often situated towards the end of the Act, these can be a useful starting point.

Legislation also includes Statutory Instruments which may be in the form of rules, regulations and orders. The term delegated legislation collectively describes this body of law as it is made under delegated authority of Parliament, usually by a minister or government department. Statutory Instruments tend to provide additional detail to the outline scheme provided by the primary legislation, the Act of Parliament. Statutory Instruments are usually cited by year and a number, for example, Local Authority Social Services (Complaints Procedure) Order SI 2006/1681.

Various documents may be issued to further assist with the implementation of legislation including guidance and codes of practice.

Guidance

Guidance documents may be described as formal or practice guidance. Formal guidance may be identified as such where it is stated to have been issued under s. 7(1) of the Local Authority Social Services Act 1970, which provides that 'local authorities shall act under the general guidance of the Secretary of State'. An example of s. 7 guidance is *Working Together to Safeguard Children* (2013, London: Department of Health). The significance of s. 7 guidance was explained by Sedley J in *R v London Borough of Islington, ex parte Rixon* [1997] ELR 66: 'Parliament in enacting s. 7(1) did not intend local authorities to whom ministerial guidance was given to be free, having considered it, to take it or leave it … in my view parliament by s. 7(1) has required local authorities to follow the path charted by the Secretary of State's guidance, with liberty to deviate from it where the local authority judges on admissible grounds that there is good reason to do so, but without freedom to take a substantially different course.' (71)

Practice guidance does not carry s. 7 status but should nevertheless normally be followed as setting examples of what good practice might look like.

Codes of practice

Codes of practice have been issued to support the Mental Health Act 1983 and the Mental Capacity Act 2005. Again, it is a matter of good practice to follow the recommendations of the codes and these lengthy documents include detailed and illustrative scenarios to assist with interpretation and application of the legislation. There may also be a duty on specific people charged with responsibilities under the primary legislation to have regard to the code.

Guidance and codes of practice are available on relevant websites, for example, the Department of Health, as referenced in individual volumes.

Case law

Case law provides a further major source of law. In determining disputes in court the judiciary applies legislation. Where provisions within legislation are unclear or ambiguous the judiciary follows principles of statutory interpretation but at times judges are quite creative.

Some areas of law are exclusively contained in case law and described as common law. Most law of relevance to social work practice is of relatively recent origin and has its primary basis in legislation. Case law remains relevant as it links directly to such legislation and may clarify and explain provisions and terminology within the legislation. The significance of a particular decision will depend on the position of the court in a hierarchy whereby the Supreme Court is most senior and the Magistrates' Court is junior. Decisions of the higher courts bind the lower courts – they must be followed. This principle is known as the doctrine of precedent. Much legal debate takes place as to the precise element of a ruling which subsequently binds other decisions. This is especially the case where in the Court of Appeal or Supreme Court there are between three and five judges hearing a case, majority judgments are allowed and different judges may arrive at the same conclusion but for different reasons. Where a judge does not agree with the majority, the term dissenting judgment is applied.

It is important to understand how cases reach court. Many cases in social work law are based on challenges to the way a local authority has exercised its powers. This is an aspect of administrative law known as judicial review where the central issue for the court is not the substance of the decision taken by the authority but the way it was taken. Important considerations will be whether the authority has exceeded its powers, failed to follow established procedures or acted irrationally.

Before an individual can challenge an authority in judicial review it will usually be necessary to exhaust other remedies first, including local authority complaints procedures. If unsatisfied with the outcome of a complaint an individual has a further option which is to complain to the local government ombudsman (LGO). The LGO investigates alleged cases of maladministration and may make recommendations to local authorities including the payment of financial compensation. Ombudsman decisions may be accessed on the LGO website and make interesting reading. In cases involving social services, a common concern across children's and adults' services is unreasonable delay in carrying out assessments and providing services. See www.lgo.org.uk.

Classification of law

The above discussion related to the sources and status of laws. It is also important to note that law can serve a variety of functions and may be grouped into recognized classifications. For law relating to social work practice key classifications distinguish between law which is criminal or civil and law which is public or private.

Whilst acknowledging the importance of these classifications, it must also be appreciated that individual concerns and circumstances may not always fall so neatly into the same categories, a given scenario may engage with criminal, civil, public and private law.

- Criminal law relates to alleged behaviour which is defined by statute or common law as an offence prosecuted by the state, carrying a penalty which may include imprisonment. The offence must be proved 'beyond reasonable doubt'.
- Civil law is the term applied to all other areas of law and often focuses on disputes between individuals. A lower standard of proof, 'balance of probabilities', applies in civil cases.
- Public law is that in which society has some interest and involves a public authority, such as care proceedings.
- Private law operates between individuals, such as marriage or contract.

Legal skills guide: accessing and understanding the law

Legislation

Legislation may be accessed as printed copies published by The Stationery Office and is also available online. Some books on a particular area of law will include a copy of the Act (sometimes anno-tated) and this is a useful way of learning about new laws. As time goes by, however, and amendments are made to legislation it can become increasingly difficult to keep track of the up-to-date version of an Act. Revised and up-to-date versions of legislation (as well as the version originally enacted) are available on the website www.legislation.gov.uk.

Legislation may also be accessed on the Parliament website. Here, it is possible to trace the progress of current and draft Bills and a link to Hansard provides transcripts of debates on Bills as they pass through both Houses of Parliament, www.parliament.uk.

Bills and new legislation are often accompanied by 'Explanatory notes' which can give some background to the development of the new law and offer useful explanations of each provision.

Case law

Important cases are reported in law reports available in traditional bound volumes (according to court, specialist area or general weekly reports) or online. Case referencing is known as citation and follows particular conventions according to whether a hard copy law report or online version is sought.

Citation of cases in law reports begins with the names of the parties, followed by the year and volume number of the law report, followed by an abbreviation of the law report title, then the page number. For example: *Lawrence v Pembrokeshire CC* [2007] 2 FLR 705. The case is reported in volume 2 of the 2007 Family Law Report at page 705.

Online citation, sometimes referred to as neutral citation because it is not linked to a particular law report, also starts with the names of the parties, followed by the year in which the case was decided, followed by an abbreviation of the court in which the case was heard, followed by a number representing the place in the order of cases decided by that court. For example: *R (Macdonald) v Royal Borough of Kensington and Chelsea* [2011] UKSC 33. Neutral citation of this case shows that it was a 2011 decision of the Supreme Court.

University libraries tend to have subscriptions to particular legal databases, such as 'Westlaw', which can be accessed by those enrolled as students, often via direct links from the university library webpage. Westlaw and LexisNexis are especially useful as sources of case law, statutes and other legal materials. Libraries usually have their own guides to these sources, again often published on their websites. For most cases there is a short summary or analysis as well as the full transcript.

As not everyone using the series will be enrolled at a university, the following website can be accessed without any subscription: BAILLI (British and Irish Legal Information Institute) www.bailii.org. This site includes judgments from the full range of UK court services including the Supreme Court, Court of Appeal and High Court but also features a wide range of tribunal decisions. Judgments for Scotland, Northern Ireland and the Republic of Ireland are also available as are judgments of the European Court of Human Rights.

Whether accessed via a law report or online, the presentation of cases follows a template. The report begins with the names of the parties, the court which heard the cases, names(s) of the judges(s) and dates of the hearing. This is followed by a summary of key legal issues involved in the case (often in italics) known as catchwords, then the headnote, which is a paragraph or so stating the key facts of the case and the nature of the claim or dispute or the criminal charge. 'HELD' indicates the ruling of the court. This is followed by a list of cases that were referred to in legal argument during the hearing, a summary of the journey of the case through appeal processes, names of the advocates and then the start of the full judgment(s) given by the judge(s). The judgment usually recounts the circumstances of the case, findings of fact and findings on the law and reasons for the decision.

If stuck on citations the Cardiff Index to Legal Abbreviations is a useful resource at www.legalabbrevs.cardiff.ac.uk.

There are numerous specific guides to legal research providing more detailed examination of legal materials but the best advice on developing legal skills is to start exploring the above and to read some case law – it's surprisingly addictive!

INTRODUCTION

AT A GLANCE THIS CHAPTER COVERS:

- the policy context
- structure of the youth justice system
- Youth Offending Teams
- the welfare principle
- children's rights
- safeguarding and child welfare
- developments under the Coalition government

Working with young people in the youth justice system is a challenging area of practice that requires a particular depth of knowledge and skill. It is an increasingly politicized area of social work, with politicians and successive governments seeking to make a visible impact (Johns, 2011), resulting in a rapidly developing body of legislation and national standards for practice. Practitioners are expected to uphold the sometimes conflicting values of both social work and youth justice and also have to balance the potential ethical and moral dilemmas within their work with young people who are involved in offending behaviour. Many of these children and young people will have caused considerable emotional, physical, financial and social harm to others, yet they demonstrate the same needs and are entitled to the same rights as all children.

There is no single piece of legislation guiding the youth justice system, but a wide range of law, both civil and criminal, that has developed in a sporadic, non-systematic manner. It is neither possible nor beneficial to attempt to cover all of the legislation, sentencing guidance and practice standards relating to specific aspects of youth justice. Rather, this book aims to provide an overview of the youth justice system, combining an explanation of the stages of the youth justice process with a focus on select key pieces of legislation, within a framework of children's rights. In this way, it aims to support students and practitioners in understanding how youth justice legislation may affect children and their families, and in achieving positive outcomes with young people at the borders of and involved in the youth justice system. Further readings are suggested at the end of each chapter should the reader wish to explore particular aspects of the system in more depth.

The policy context

Youth justice policy and practice operates within a complex framework of legal, moral, ethical and professional standards, academic research, criminological theories and philosophies of childhood, within a wider context of political, social and economic pressures, and is thus constantly in flux. Responses to young people involved in offending behaviour are situated within perpetual arguments about the nature of childhood and contrary conceptualizations of children – as 'devils or angels' (Fionda, 2005), innocent or knowing; these contrasting notions have challenged scholars and policy-makers for centuries, being influenced by religion, philanthropy, science and social development (see, for example,

Cunningham, 2006). The dominant concepts of childhood have varied across time and thereby affected the construction and implementation of legal (and moral) standards regarding children's behaviour since the development of a distinct youth justice system in the early twentieth century. The most persistent themes apparent within literature on the evolution of youth justice legislation surround taxonomies of 'welfare' or 'justice', or 'need' versus 'risk' (Crawford and Newburn, 2003; Pickford and Dugmore, 2012; Fox and Arnull, 2013) – the welfare and needs of the young offender versus the risk to society and the desire for justice for victims. However, these dichotomies over-simplify the complexity of both historical and current responses to offending behaviour by young people and the construction of the youth justice system is significantly more convoluted.

At its heart, the youth justice system highlights the tensions between the competing aims of legislative sanctioning for offending or antisocial behaviour – whether the justice system aims to provide deterrence, incapacitation, retribution, or rehabilitation (Fionda, 2005), or some combination of these goals. The lack of a single, clear objective is similarly apparent within the adult justice system but the issue is further complicated within youth justice due to the perception of children and young people as less culpable than adults, while also being more malleable and open to rehabilitation. The **Youth Justice Board** for England and Wales (YJB) states that the primary purpose of the youth justice system is to 'prevent offending' (Crime and Disorder Act (CDA) 1998; discussed below), but does not specify whether this should be through deterrence, incapacitation, retribution, rehabilitation or some other measure. This uncertainty of purpose is exacerbated by political ambitions that have, both concurrently and cyclically:

- imposed a managerialist drive for cost-efficiency (**managerialism**) through systems-management and actuarialism, through a focus on evidence-based practice, the systematic measurement and monitoring of processes and practice, and the development of key performance indicators;
- sought to assuage public concern about perceived levels of youth crime through popular punitivism and harsh sentencing practices;
- responded to practitioners' and academics' concerns by diverting young people from the potentially **criminogenic** influence of the youth justice process itself through a twin-track system of bifurcation;

- tried to eliminate discrepancies in sentencing responses by introducing just deserts measures and proportionality;
- extended the focus of youth justice to include preventionism, remoralization and responsibilization;
- more recently, introduced a **scaled approach** to sentencing, with increasing levels of intervention for successive offences.

The means of achieving, and measuring, each of these outcomes may differ widely and, in some instances, directly conflict, resulting in a complex and contradictory range of responses to youth offending.

The youth justice system

The youth justice system is thus comprised of elements of this 'meze' (Fionda, 2005), or 'smorgasbord' (Pickford and Dugmore, 2012) of different approaches to youth offending, reflecting the constantly shifting agenda of youth justice legislation (Muncie and Hughes, 2002). The New Labour government significantly reformed the structure of the youth justice system, guided by five key (but not necessarily complementary) principles:

- the primacy of offending prevention;
- the responsibilization of children and their parents;
- the use of reparation as a tangible manifestation of an offender's willingness to take responsibility for an offence and also as evidence of a commitment to prioritize the needs of victims;
- early, effective and progressive intervention; and
- efficiency – speeding up the system to reduce delays for victims and offenders and to reduce costs.

These principles were reflected in six key themes within the CDA 1998, explored throughout this book:

- the primary aim of the youth justice system is to prevent offending (s. 37; see Chapter 1);
- partnership and multi-agency working (s. 39; see below);
- tackling offending behaviour and providing early intervention (s. 11, s. 14, s. 65, s. 69; see Chapter 1);
- a focus on reparation (s. 67; see Chapter 4);
- a focus on parenting (s. 8; see Chapter 1);
- more effective custodial sentences (s. 73; see Chapter 5).

The CDA 1998 established multi-agency **Youth Offending Teams** (YOTs) to work with children and young people aged 10–17. Local authorities have significant responsibilities relating to crime prevention and developing annual youth justice plans but the primary operational responsibility for delivering services was assigned to YOTs under the CDA 1998 (as amended by the Offender Management Act 2007 and Criminal Justice and Immigration Act (CJIA) 2008; see also Johns, 2011). Section 41 CDA 1998 also created the YJB, whose role is to: advise the Justice Secretary on how to effectively pursue the principal aim of preventing offending; encourage and monitor nationwide consistency through a National Framework for youth justice, national standards and the promotion of good practice; oversee the provision of services; and commission and manage the juvenile secure estate.

Youth Offending Teams

The constituent membership of YOTs varies but, as Fox and Arnull (2013) detail, YOT staff may include:

- police officers – most likely to be involved in administering cautions and pre-court diversionary activities, but may also supervise young people serving community sentences;
- probation officers – usually aim to work with 16–18-year-olds, although in practice may have a broader remit (roles include conducting assessments, writing **pre-sentence reports** (PSRs) and supervising community sentences);
- youth workers – were expected to be included in all YOTs but many do not have them, partly due to financial constraints, but also due to the professional view that some youth services have taken in recognition of the voluntary nature of their engagement with young people;
- health professionals – were expected to play a major role within YOTs but this has varied; in some areas specialist treatment such as substance misuse or mental health treatment is provided, others provide a referral route to specialist support such as educational psychology, Child and Adolescent Mental Health Services, or speech and language therapy. Health professionals also have a more generic role undertaking health assessments;
- education, training and employment advisors – were provided by Connexions but are now provided in different forms;

- housing – some areas have dedicated housing support and advice either within the YOT or via a nominated person within the local housing service;
- specialists in identified areas from either the statutory or voluntary sectors, for example, mental health or substance abuse support. The specialist advice and support that each team has varies, as each is a product of its own local services and is 'owned' by those services.

YOTs vary in size, from less than 20 members of staff (including volunteers, part-time and temporary staff) to over 500 (Ministry of Justice (MoJ), 2013a). The variation is a reflection of local need and political priorities and the effectiveness of senior strategic relationships (Fox and Arnull, 2013). Initially, members of the YOT were to be seconded in from their organization for a specified period of time, but in practice they often remained part of the YOT rather than returning to their original position (Souhami, 2008).

YOT staff may be involved in completing assessments, writing presentence or sentence-specific reports, attending court, supervising young people on orders, running interventions to prevent offending, working with families, liaising with victims, chairing **referral order** panels, supporting young people on release from custody and so on. In some YOTs, staff will have designated roles (report writer, court officer, supervising officer), while in others individuals may be involved in some or all of these activities; practitioners therefore may develop a range of generic and specialist skills, requiring an understanding of all areas of youth justice legislation.

The welfare principle

The 'welfare principle' underpins all legal responses to youth offending, enacted in the Children and Young Persons Act (CYPA) 1933:

s. 44

(1) Every court in dealing with a child or young person who is brought before it, either as an offender or otherwise, shall have regard to the welfare of the child or young person and shall in a proper case take steps for removing him from undesirable surroundings, and for securing that proper provision is made for his education and training.

CYPA 1933

The welfare principle clearly establishes a legal standard that all youth justice interventions should adhere to, based on the recognition that all children, including those who offend, may be vulnerable and are still developing, and that the state, as the guardian of its citizens, has a paternalistic duty towards children (Pickford and Dugmore, 2012). This welfare-based approach underpinned much subsequent legislation (including the Children Act 1948, Children and Young Persons (Amendment) Act 1952, Children and Young Persons Act 1963 and the Children and Young Persons Act 1969), but became less prominent in youth justice legislation towards the end of the twentieth century. However, it was re-emphasized in the Children Act 1989 (s. 1: 'The child's welfare shall be the court's paramount consideration.') and the Children Act 2004, which stipulates that YOTs have a statutory duty to make arrangements for ensuring that 'their functions are discharged having regard to the need to safeguard and promote the welfare of children'.

How the welfare of the child is balanced with the requirements of the youth justice system is far from clear-cut. Case law has reinforced the need to adhere to the welfare principle in relation to children in the youth justice system (Howard League for Penal Reform, 2013), for example, in *R (M) v Chief Magistrate* [2010], it was stated that: 'The welfare of the child is an important and indeed fundamental consideration in determining how a child who has committed offences should be dealt with.' However, this still has to be interpreted in conjunction with the relevant criminal justice statutes and guidance, such as that issued by the Sentencing Council.

Children's rights

The United Nations Convention on the Rights of the Child

The United Nations Convention on the Rights of the Child 1989 (UNCRC) and associated guidance attempt to protect the rights of children and young people involved in offending behaviour. Article 2 UNCRC provides that all of the rights guaranteed by the Convention must be available to all children without discrimination of any kind. Article 40(3) states that children in conflict with the law have the right to be treated:

> … in a manner consistent with the promotion of the child's sense of dignity and worth, which reinforces the child's respect for the human rights and fundamental freedoms of others and which

takes into account the child's age and the desirability of promoting the child's reintegration and the child's assuming a constructive role in society. (Article 2 UNCRC)

In addition to the UNCRC, the operation of the youth justice system should abide by the wide range of international instruments that have either general or specific reference to children in conflict with the law. These include agreements that are binding on states and non-binding statements of best practice encompassing the whole of the youth justice system, from early intervention and diversion, fair trial and justice issues, through to detention and the re-integration of the young person into society, and include:

- United Nations (UN) Standard Minimum Rules for the Protection of Juvenile Justice 1985 (Beijing Rules);
- UN Rules for Protection of Juveniles Deprived of their Liberty 1990 (Havana Rules);
- UN Guidelines for the Administration of Juvenile Delinquency 1990 (Riyadh Guidelines);
- European Convention on Human Rights 1953 (ECHR);
- European Rules for Juvenile Offenders Subject to Sanctions or Measures (Council of Europe 2009);
- Guidelines of the Committee of Ministers of the Council of Europe on Child-Friendly Justice (Council of Europe 2010).

Some, but crucially not all, of the rights within these treaties are enacted within domestic legislation in the guise of the Children Act 1989 and the Human Rights Act 1998. However, aspects of the youth justice system – such as the low minimum age of criminal responsibility (MACR) and the abolition of **doli incapax** (see key case analysis), some interventions to 'prevent' offending, the abolition of the right to silence, the trial of children as adults within the Crown Court, and the detention of children (all discussed later in this book) – breach the rights granted to children under the UNCRC and associated guidance. The failure to fully incorporate the UNCRC into domestic legislation has generated wide-spread condemnation, not only from the UN Committee on the Rights of the Child, which is tasked with monitoring compliance with the provisions and protocols of the UNCRC, but also from academics, criminal justice organizations and children's rights groups (see, for example, Children's Rights Alliance for England (CRAE), 2013).

→ **KEY CASE ANALYSIS** ←

R v T [2008]: The abolition of doli incapax and the age of criminal responsibility

The MACR in England and Wales is 10; this is significantly lower than the average MACR across Western Europe and contradicts the granting of autonomy within civil statute (the age of sexual consent, voting, smoking, drinking alcohol, marriage, driving and so on). Until 1998, the low MACR was perhaps mitigated by the doctrine of *doli incapax* – the rebuttable principle that provided a legal safeguard for children aged 10 to 14 by requiring the prosecution to prove that the child fully understood the legal, moral and social implications of their offending behaviour. However, strongly influenced by popular punitivism, concerns about 'feral' youth and the desire to make children accountable for their behaviour, the principle of *doli incapax* was abolished by s. 34 CDA 1998, perhaps one of the biggest indicators of the new responsibilization agenda. The abolition of *doli incapax* was questioned by Smith LJ in *Director of Public Prosecutions v P* [2007] (a case involving a 13-year-old child with attention deficit hyperactivity disorder (ADHD) and a low intelligence quotient (IQ)), but was confirmed by the Court of Appeal in *R v T* [2008], when a 12-year-old boy was charged with 12 counts of causing or inciting a child under 13 to engage in sexual activity. The Court of Appeal was convinced that s. 34 CDA 1998 abolished not only the presumption of *doli incapax* but the whole doctrine, such that from the age of 10 a child is fully responsible for his or her actions (Crofts, 2009). Although age may be used to mitigate the sentence passed, it is no longer considered a factor in culpability.

The MACR has remained unchanged since 1963, despite considerable developments in the understanding of children's psychological maturation and children's rights (see further reading, below). Both the UNCRC 1989 and the Beijing Rules 1985 recognize the fundamental importance of the age-appropriate treatment of children, including establishing an age of criminal responsibility below which children will be presumed not to have the capacity to infringe the criminal law – taking into account their likely emotional, mental and intellectual maturity. The UN Committee on the Rights of the Child (2007) strongly recommends that the age of criminal responsibility should be at least 12 years, and ideally 14–16 years. However, despite widespread consensus that the MACR should be raised, there is no legal venue in which the legitimacy of the MACR can be challenged; the only possibility of change lies with successive governments, none of which have so far been prepared to consider progressive reform.

The Human Rights Act 1998

The Human Rights Act 1998, incorporating the ECHR, perhaps provides more legal recourse for children and young people than the UNCRC; ultimately breaches of these rights can be appealed within the court system – although there are concerns about the ability of children and young people to seek independent legal redress, particularly in light of reforms to legal aid (Coram Children's Legal Centre, 2013). Courts have also held that the rights set out in the ECHR can be read in light of the rights in the UNCRC and other equivalent, non-binding international law. For instance, if a child's application for early release from custody is impossible because of a lack of resettlement plans, the interference with that child's right to liberty under Article 5 ECHR is especially serious as there is a duty under Article 37 UNCRC to make sure that children are detained for the shortest appropriate period of time (Howard League for Penal Reform, 2013). Such breaches will be discussed throughout this book, highlighting the challenges for professionals working with children and young people involved in offending behaviour.

Safeguarding and child welfare

In addition to children's rights legislation, youth justice practitioners also need an understanding of child welfare legislation and safeguarding procedures; YOTs are required to be part of Local Safeguarding Children Boards (LSCBs), both strategically and operationally (see Department for Education, 2013; Ball, 2014). Of particular relevance to those working in multi-agency YOTs are *Every Child Matters* (Department for Children Schools and Families (DCSF), 2003) and the Children Act 2004, which established Children's Trusts, creating a multi-agency forum to coordinate the activities of children's social services departments, community and acute health services and local education authorities. As with YOTs, these multi-agency teams were developed to provide a more holistic response to children, allowing for joint training, better information-sharing and the implementation of the Common Assessment Framework (now replaced by the Single Assessment Framework (SAF)). It is of note, however, that there was little done to promote horizontal coordination across the two jurisdictions (Cavadino, et al., 2013), such that there is considerable overlap between, for example, the work of youth justice-based early intervention projects that use the **ONSET** assessment framework and welfare-based multi-agency panels that use SAF, with many children being subject to both forms of assessment and intervention (see Chapter 1).

It is somewhat nonsensical that successive governments have encouraged multi-agency working and improved communication when working with children yet perpetuate the difficulties by dividing the responsibility for young offenders and 'other' children at a ministerial level. Whilst the duty for child welfare rests with the Department for Education, the youth justice system falls within the remit of the MoJ, with their competing legal frameworks of child welfare and youth justice (Fox and Arnull, 2013). The apparent structural dominance of the justice system over the welfare system reflects the differentiation between 'troublesome' and 'troubled' children. This division was visible within *Every Child Matters* itself (DCSF, 2003), which, while arguing that *every* child matters, had a separate, accompanying document for young offenders (*Youth Justice: The Next Steps,* Home Office, 2003), implicitly suggesting that children and young people who offend somehow matter less than other children. Thus the politicization of crime and welfare continues to differentiate how services are viewed and deployed.

Developments under the Coalition government

Many of the New Labour reforms still exist, but the Coalition government has made some significant changes to the structure and operation of the youth justice system. For example, the Coalition government has brought the YJB under greater control from the MoJ, to increase ministerial responsibility and to oversee key issues that have a 'reputational impact', despite arguments from a number of agencies that the political impartiality of the YJB should be maintained (MoJ, 2013b).

The Coalition government has also made moves to expand restorative justice measures (particularly pre-court and diversionary interventions) and to free up agencies from central control (in contrast to the centralizing, coordinating thrust of New Labour's neo-correctionalism). However, it is questionable whether the Coalition rhetoric about encouraging more informal interventions and increasing restorative justice is being driven by a perceived need to reduce expenditure rather than a real desire to be less punitive. The reduction in YOTs' budgets since 2006 (including a reduction of 12 per cent from 2010/2011 to 2011/2012 alone: MoJ, 2013a), combined with the introduction of Children's Trusts, mean that the overall level of staffing in YOTs decreased by 15 per cent over the same period (MoJ, 2013a). If YOT capacity is diminished, there is a likelihood that YOTs will have to make more referrals into mainstream services, thus affecting local authority children's services (Fox and Arnull, 2013). The increased need to do more with less may not correlate with the desired goal of partnership and collaborative working that underpins much recent legislation and guidance (Fox and Arnull, 2013). Furthermore, outsourcing elements of the youth justice system to voluntary agencies, using unqualified sessional workers and volunteers to deliver services, runs counter to the emphasis on evidence-based practice and the professionalization of youth justice work encouraged by the YJB.

Payment-by-results

The Coalition government promised a 'rehabilitation revolution' in the Green Paper *Breaking the Cycle* (MoJ, 2010), combining the Conservative belief in the privatization of public services with the enthusiasm for reforming offenders revived by New Labour (Cavadino et al., 2013). The proposals include the part-privatization of some youth justice services and the introduction of a 'payment-by-results' approach to both adult and youth reoffending work. Pilot studies of payment-by-results have been implemented in the adult justice system, whereby agencies with responsibility for offenders are paid more for producing lower reoffending rates. Arguably, such schemes could lead to a significant reduction in reoffending rates and, thereby, considerable savings on reconvicting and re-imprisoning offenders, as well as reduced victimization (although, as noted earlier, the government appears to be driven more by financial concerns than by the needs or rights of stakeholders within the justice process). It is early yet to judge the results of these schemes but there are concerns that the approach may be over-optimistic – whilst *some* interventions can claim modest reductions in reoffending compared with other measures for *some* offenders, it is difficult to maintain significant relative success rates with any type of intervention (see Bottoms, 2004). The payment-by-results strategy presupposes that criminal justice agencies, including those in the private and voluntary sectors, will be adept at identifying and implementing effective rather than ineffective rehabilitation programmes: 'given the still primitive nature of knowledge about how to reform offenders, such an assumption requires quite a leap of faith' (Cavadino et al., 2013:41). There are pragmatic concerns over how crossovers between different providers (with potentially very different business or social objectives) will be managed and coordinated (Hudson, 2013). It is also unclear how effectiveness is to be defined or measured, how payment is to be made to the various agencies that might have been involved, and when payments would be made – many interventions are long-term and seldom have a clear-cut binary outcome (Fox and Albertson, 2011; Hudson, 2013). Developing a contract culture, with micro-management of targets, rigid monitoring systems and so forth, places agencies under pressure to act as low-cost providers, rather than enabling them to become exemplars of innovative practice. It is also possible that providers will only want to work with those presenting the best chances of success, leaving state providers to work with children and young people with the most complex, entrenched difficulties.

Conclusions

The joined-up approach created by New Labour is arguably a 'smorgasbord' combination of different philosophical, political and professional approaches to youth justice, but appears to have had a significant impact on decreasing the numbers of children drawn into the youth justice system and on reducing the juvenile custodial population (see Chapter 1). There is a risk that maximizing private-sector involvement will dismantle this joined-up approach, fragmenting the system through part-privatization and payment-by-results (Cavadino et al., 2013). Those working within the system face the challenges of maintaining the reduction in the youth justice population and protecting and promoting the rights of children and young people involved in the system, within ongoing financial constraints and a public attitude that can be hostile towards children whose behaviour transgresses accepted social boundaries. The next chapter considers the identification of those seen to be 'at risk' of involvement in offending behaviour and introduces the **risk, needs and responsivity** framework that underpins current youth justice responses. The chapter gives a brief overview of statistical information on youth offending and reflects on public views of young offenders before outlining quasi-legal measures and civil law responses to anti-social behaviour, including early intervention and prevention programmes. Chapter 2 discusses the powers of the police towards young people involved in offending behaviour, before court structures and processes are discussed in Chapter 3. The community and custodial sentences available for young people are outlined in Chapters 4 and 5, respectively. The final chapter reflects on tensions for professionals working with young offenders and the need to uphold children's rights throughout their involvement in the youth justice system.

Further reading

Cavadino, M, J Dignan and G Mair (2013) *The Penal System: An Introduction* presents a comprehensive, accessible overview of the development and characteristics of the English penal system, with a specific chapter on the youth justice system.

Fionda, J (2005) *Devils or Angels: Youth, Policy and Crime* considers the criminalization of children's behaviour and the negative public image that creates a fear and distrust of children and young people. Fionda reflects on the failure of social policy to address factors influencing offending behaviour and compares this with welfare-based interventions in other European jurisdictions.

United Nations Children's Fund (UNICEF) (2013) provides an overview of the UNCRC and associated rules, guidance, principles and state obligations. See www.unicef.org/crc.

Youth Justice (2013) 13(2): this special issue of the journal focuses specifically on the MACR and features a number of articles analysing the need to raise the MACR from medical, legal, social and psychological perspectives.

1

UNDERSTANDING AND PREVENTING OFFENDING BEHAVIOUR

AT A GLANCE THIS CHAPTER COVERS:

- the extent of youth offending
- risk, needs and responsivity and the scaled approach
- community-based prevention and early intervention programmes
- civil legislation
- anti-social behaviour
- gang injunctions
- discrimination and rights

Every local authority has a duty under s. 37 CDA 1998 to work towards the reduction of crime and disorder, with an explicit emphasis on preventing offending by children and young people. This is echoed in the YJB's *National Standards for Youth Justice Services* (2013a) with National Standard 1: 'Preventing Offending' stipulating that local strategies and services are established to prevent children and young people from becoming involved in crime and/or anti-social behaviour, and to support their parents/carers and families. The use of preventative and diversionary measures is emphasized by the UNCRC 1989, recognizing that such measures can be cost effective by avoiding the need for full judicial proceedings, reducing stigmatization, and having beneficial outcomes for children. However, such programmes must ensure that children's rights and safeguards are fully respected. For example, individual orders should only be used where there is convincing evidence that the child is involved in or has been clearly identified as being at risk of involvement in offending or anti-social behaviour, where they acknowledge responsibility and give consent, and where the acknowledgment will not be used against them in any subsequent legal proceedings.

The chapter begins with a consideration of the extent of youth offending and the public perception of youth crime to provide a context for reflecting on formal responses to unwanted behaviour. It addresses the focus on the assessment of '**risk factors**' for involvement in offending or anti-social behaviour, the development of **ASSET** and **ASSETPlus**, and the scaled approach to youth justice interventions. Consideration is then given to the YJB's Youth Crime Prevention Strategy and wider community-based prevention initiatives such as the Troubled Families Programme, Sure Start, Children's Centres and parenting support programmes, which, whilst having a broader remit, aim also to prevent involvement in offending and anti-social behaviour. Although not part of the youth justice system per se, these interventions are often a precursor to civil legal measures implemented to combat early involvement in offending behaviour, such as injunctions to prevent nuisance and annoyance (IPNAs), curfew orders and dispersal orders, which are then discussed.

The extent of youth offending

Official statistics typically underestimate the extent of offending behaviour, because unreported offending behaviour cannot be included, but in general they do correlate well with self-reported offending behaviour by children and young people, which consistently shows that approximately 25 per cent of young people admit to involvement in anti-social or offending behaviour in the previous 12 months (Halsey and White, undated). Conversely, official statistics are likely to overestimate the proportion of crime that can be attributed to young people as such figures tend to exclude 'white-collar' crime and offences committed by corporate bodies or the state; young people's behaviour is also more visible and more closely monitored (by parents, teachers, security staff and community members, as well as by the police) than that of older people, resulting in an increased focus on youth offending.

It is very difficult to unpick changes and patterns in youth offending behaviour and distinguish 'real' changes from those that result from a change in recording practice, police action, or sentencing policy. For example, from 1992–2003 there was a significant decline in detected youth crime but this was apparently reversed between 2003–2008 (Pickford and Dugmore, 2012). However, much of this reversal can be related to changes in police practice due to the Labour government's target to increase offences brought to justice (OBTJ) (also known as 'sanction detections'), rather than because there was a genuine increase in youth offending (MoJ, 2013a). To meet the OBTJ targets, many police forces focused, in particular, on less serious offences committed by young people – those offences easiest to pursue and detect – resulting in an apparent increase in youth crime, especially that committed by girls. Once the target was removed, declines in youth crime, particularly offences committed by first-time offenders, were notable. Indeed, the number of first-time entrants to the youth justice system fell by 75 per cent from a peak of over 110,000 in 2006/2007, to 27,854 in 2012/2013 (MoJ, 2014) (See Figure 1.1).

In 2011/2012 there were 167,995 arrests of young people aged 10–17 for **notifiable offences** (MoJ, 2014), accounting for 13.6 per cent of all arrests; those aged 10–17 make up only 10.8 per cent of the population of England and Wales, suggesting that young people are over-represented in the criminal justice system. The majority of arrests of young people were of boys (11.3 per cent of all arrests), with just 2.3 per cent of all arrests being girls aged 10–17. The number of young people who are diverted from the youth justice system through triage or other diversionary processes is not known, but police contact with children

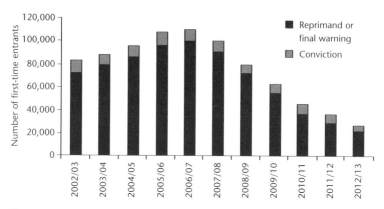

Figure 1.1: Trends in first-time entrants to the youth justice system, 2002/2003–2012/2013

Source: Ministry of Justice/Youth Justice Board, 2014

and young people in 2012/2013 led to 30,778 reprimands, final warnings or conditional cautions being given, a reduction of 64 per cent since 2002/2003 (MoJ, 2014). There were 98,837 proven offences by young people in 2012/2013; a decrease of 28 per cent from the previous year (MoJ, 2014); the majority (77 per cent) of these were committed by young people aged over 15, and by boys (82 per cent). Almost 44,000 young people were sentenced at all criminal courts in 2012/2013, 28 per cent fewer than the year before (MoJ, 2014); the sentences received are discussed in subsequent chapters.

The most common offences committed by young people are violence against the person (including common assault) (21 per cent), theft and handling (19 per cent), and criminal damage (11 per cent). More serious offences, such as sexual offending, are rarer with less than 2 per cent of proven offences committed by young people in 2012/2013 being sexual offences (MoJ, 2014).

On-the-spot questions

1 Why is it important to measure the extent of youth crime?
2 Why is measuring the extent of youth crime problematic?

Public perceptions of youth offending

Although the number of offences committed by young people and the number of young people involved in the youth justice system appear to be decreasing, research suggests that the public perceive youth offending to be increasing and the fear of youth crime remains high (Hough and Roberts, 2004; Pickford and Dugmore, 2012). Any work conducted with young people involved in the youth justice system is thus set against a backdrop of public antipathy, and sometimes hostility, towards children and young people (Hough and Roberts, 2004; Ipsos MORI, 2006). For example, the Crime Survey for England and Wales (formally the British Crime Survey) includes a question (within the sub-section on anti-social behaviour) about 'teenagers hanging around on the streets', suggesting that such behaviour is inherently negative. This raises questions about children and young people's right to free assembly and appropriate provision for children and young people. The UN Committee on the Rights of the Child (2008) expressed significant concern at the 'general climate of intolerance and negative public attitudes towards children, especially adolescents, which appears to exist in the UK, including in the media', and put forward almost 120 recommendations on how to improve children's rights in the UK in general, including reducing the intolerance shown towards children and young people.

On-the-spot question	How do public perceptions of youth crime influence the development of policy and legislation?

Characteristics of known young offenders

Positivist research by a number of academics and organizations (for example, Rutter et al., 1998; Hagell, 2002; Hammersley et al., 2003; HM Inspectorate of Prisons, 2003; Arnull et al., 2005; YJB, 2005; Farrington and Welsh, 2007) has identified a range of social, biological and structural factors common to those involved, or seen at risk of being involved, in offending behaviour – some of which are considered within the ASSET/ASSETPlus frameworks developed by the YJB. Such characteristics may be static factors – including gender, a history of offending within the family, abuse or loss, brain trauma and pre-natal difficulties such as foetal alcohol syndrome – whilst others are (or can be) dynamic factors – such as the experience of poverty, negative peer relationships, inconsistent parenting, low educational attainment and/or non-attendance at school, mental health difficulties, or substance misuse. It is not yet fully under-stood how or why combinations of factors result in offending behaviour (Fox and Arnull, 2013), but it is known that many of the risk factors are inter-related – for example, the risk factors associated with mental health problems and offending correlate and overlap (Khan, 2010), and those for youth offending are largely similar to those for educational under-achievement (YJB, 2005). Many of these factors are exacerbated by indi-vidual and structural discrimination. For example, approximately one-fifth of young people in custody have some form of learning disabil-ity (Bryan et al., 2007); and many young people with learning difficulties come from lower socioeconomic backgrounds, which can further exac-erbate the problems they experience (Fyson and Yates, 2011; Fox and Arnull, 2013), resulting in their over-representation within the youth justice system. Similarly, the over-representation of black and minority ethnic young people in custody may be exacerbated because there are also disproportionate numbers of black and minority ethnic males with mental health problems and learning disabilities (Fox and Arnull, 2013).

Risk, needs and responsivity, and the scaled approach

A plethora of theories of youth offending exist, from early theories of clas-sicist notions of free will to cultural explanations (see, for example, Newburn, 2013); currently, individualistic, positivist theories of crime causation are dominant within youth justice policies and legislation. This is demonstrated through the focus on early intervention and the belief that it is possible to identify those young people who are at risk of offending and/or of causing serious harm to others, based on the characteristics iden-tified above. This has led to investment in actuarial risk prediction devices, aimed at identifying both the risk of reoffending and the risk of causing serious harm (Baker, 2005). Within the CDA 1998 and subsequent legisla-tion, New Labour prioritized and promoted a risk-based approach, with an emphasis on the prevention of offending through a multi-modal method of working (Fox and Arnull, 2013). The Coalition government continued the focus on identification, targeting and early intervention within the Social Justice Strategy (Department for Work and Pensions, 2012).

The scaled approach

The scaled approach to sentencing (discussed further in Chapter 4) has replaced proportionality of sentencing with progressive interventions of increasing intensiveness for each successive offence (Cavadino et al., 2013) and is underpinned by the risk, needs and responsivity framework. It incorporates the use of a national assessment tool commissioned by the YJB and is based on three principles:

1 the risk principle – the most intensive interventions should be reserved for those posing the highest risk of **recidivism**;
2 the needs principle – interventions should target the needs or issues most associated with the perceived causes of the particular offending behaviour;
3 the responsivity principle – planned interventions should take into account the characteristics of the young person, including their age, gender, ethnicity, personality, motivation and ability, to facilitate a positive response.

This approach explicitly links the risk assessment score to the nature, frequency, intensity and duration of subsequent interventions (CJIA 2008). The appropriate level of YOT intervention (standard, enhanced or intensive) is decided primarily on assessments of the likelihood of re-offending and the risk of serious harm posed to others, as identified through the national assessment tools.

Risk assessments – ONSET, ASSET and ASSETPlus

Despite criticisms of positivist approaches (see Newburn, 2013), the ONSET and ASSET assessment tools were developed by the YJB, under-pinned by **risk and protective factor** research (YJB, 2005); these tools have recently been reviewed and a new model, ASSETPlus, is due for national implementation in 2014/2015 (YJB, 2013b). These assessment tools ask practitioners to consider the impact of a range of risk factors, divided into family, community, school and personal/individual factors, which may be either static (for example, having previously been looked after) or dynamic (Baker et al., 2011; see also Fox and Arnull, 2013). ASSETPlus aims to provide a single 'end-to-end' dynamic assessment and plan for a young person that follows them through the youth justice system, from pre-court diversionary work through to custody (YJB, 2013b). The scope of ASSETPlus has expanded considerably, reflecting developments in research, to include speech, language and communication needs, gangs and gang-associated behaviours, the (inappropriate) use of technology, and to have an increased focus on factors for and against desistance, reflecting the *Every Child Matters* 2003 and Children

Act 2004 agenda of achieving positive outcomes for all children (Fox and Arnull, 2013). ASSETPlus also aims to be alert to the risks of a young person being vulnerable to sexual exploitation, although it is couched in terms of their susceptibility to being influenced by others.

These assessment tools are then used to identify children who reach a (variable) threshold for prevention and early intervention programmes (discussed below); determining the level of intervention necessary within the scaled approach (Chapter 4); planning, delivering and monitoring interventions for young people; and assessing the possibility of the young person causing serious psychological or physical harm to someone, thus triggering Multi-Agency Public Protection Arrangements (MAPPA) (Chapter 4).

There has been considerable criticism of basing youth justice interventions on a system of risk assessments, rather than on a deeper understanding of individual circumstances. Risk-based approaches have been criticized for being reductionist, generalist and ambiguous (Case, 2007; Bateman, 2009; Case and Haines, 2009). It is questionable whether it is either possible or appropriate to reduce young people's lives to simple, calculable risk factors or whether such risk factors can be generalized to all young people, regardless of gender, age, culture, background or lifestyle (Pickford and Dugmore, 2012). Any assessment of risk is based on probability; while assessment tools may be relatively accurate in identifying risk across a particular group of young people, tools such as ASSET have a predictive accuracy of only 60–70 per cent in regard to a specific, individual young person (YJB, 2008a). Perhaps more fundamentally, there is debate as to what is a 'risk factor' (a cause, correlate, symptom, predictor) and what is being predicted – general delinquency, anti-social behaviour, low-level or serious offending, or reoffending? High risk scores may be due to high welfare needs (Pickford and Dugmore, 2012), or be the result of structural factors, such as poverty or discrimination (Smith, 2007); the deterministic focus on positivist risk factors fails to account for individual agency, societal or cultural contexts (O'Mahoney, 2009; Paylor, 2010). Furthermore, Pickford and Dugmore (2012, drawing on Howe, 1996) argue that a risk-based justice system has become more performance-orientated, with a shift in focus from understanding to auditing, where, rather than addressing the causes of difficult behaviour, the young person is taught to 'manage' it. Professionals need to move beyond collecting and recording data, as set out by procedural guidance, and learn how to analyse and interpret the assessments so that they can understand, challenge and help young people to change (Munro, 2011). Achieving a good assessment and planning, delivering and monitoring a targeted intervention plan is dependent on the practitioner's skills and their ability to make a professional judgement based on knowledge of youth justice theory, research and practice (YJB, 2013b).

In a move that may go some way to addressing the division between welfare and justice requirements, the YJB (2013b) argues that ASSETPlus allows a more holistic assessment to be conducted and that practitioners can identify young people's needs as well as risks associated with further offending, rather than just those needs directly linked with the potential for further offending (as with the original ASSET/ONSET frameworks). However, there is no expectation that YOTs should take on more work with young people to address identified welfare needs – young people still need to be referred to universal services and other agencies to meet their welfare concerns (YJB, 2013b). Such services and organizations may struggle to manage an increase in referrals from local YOTs and caution is needed to ensure such referrals are not lost within the process.

Community-based prevention and early intervention programmes

The focus on prevention and early intervention has led to the rapid growth of the youth justice 'industry' (Pickford and Dugmore, 2012), a range of initiatives directed at young people on the fringes of offending behaviour, with the aim of diverting them from offending and promoting social inclusion (Cavadino et al., 2013). While outwith the youth justice system itself, an understanding of this provision is important as these pre-emptive interventions contribute to YOTs' target to reduce the number of first-time entrants into the criminal justice system and are often pre-cursors to civil and criminal proceedings. Many of these projects are run by voluntary and third-sector organizations, initially partly funded by the YJB through now-defunct prevention grants, through the Department for Education, police and crime commissioners or other local partners, or other funding streams (such as Neighbourhood Renewal). *Every Child Matters* (DCSF, 2003) and the addendum, *Youth Justice: The Next Steps* (Home Office, 2003), promoted a 'whole family' approach to preventing offending behaviour, with an emphasis on the accountability and responsibility of parents for their children, which has been incorporated into some of these intervention programmes. There follows a summary of the most widespread and lasting schemes.

- *Youth Inclusion Programmes* (YIPS) – Operating in a hundred of the most deprived/high-crime neighbourhoods in England and Wales, YIPs provide targeted support to 8–17-year-olds who are at high risk of involvement in crime or anti-social behaviour. Young people referred to the YIP are identified through a number of different agencies, including YOTs, police or police and community support officers (PCSOs), local authority children's and family services, local education authorities and schools (YJB, 2008b).

- *Youth Inclusion and Support Panels* (YISPs) aim to prevent anti-social behaviour and offending by children aged 8–13 years (up to 17 in some areas) who are considered to be at high risk of offending and anti-social behaviour. They are multi-agency planning groups that offer early intervention, including parenting support programmes and family group conferencing, based on assessed risk and need. Whilst there were at one time approximately 220 YISPs nationally, many have been subsumed within other local authority multi-agency partnerships (such as SAF multi-agency partnerships) to minimize the overlap between such panels, both in terms of expenditure and intervention in children's and their families' lives, as many children may have been subject to both SAF and YISP interventions (Walker et al., 2008).

- *Safer Schools Partnerships* (SSPs) constitute a formal agreement between the police and a school or cluster of schools to work together to reduce crime and the fear of crime, and to improve behaviour in and around the school, by stationing a police officer or PCSO in a school on a full or part-time basis. The underlying assumption is that, by reducing bullying, truancy and exclusions from school, SSPs will impact indirectly on offending and anti-social behaviour. They aim to intervene early with children and young people at risk of offending, improve relations between pupils, the police and the wider community, and support schools in improving pupil behaviour and attendance (DCSF et al., 2009).

- *Family Intervention Projects* were developed from the Labour government's anti-social behaviour strategy and established in many areas to provide support to families with complex needs, where other services had struggled to engage the family and/or where enforcement action was pending (such as eviction, criminal or care proceedings). These schemes led to the development of the Coalition's Troubled Families Programme, a £600m payment-by-results programme, launched in March 2012. The programme aims to enable local authorities to bring together adult and children's services to form an integrated, intensive and holistic 'whole family' approach to support the most 'troubled' families in England. These families are identified as having no working adult in the family, problematic school attendance and involvement in offending and anti-social behaviour. They may have long-standing and complex problems, including alcohol and drug abuse, domestic violence and sexual abuse, relationship breakdown, mental and physical ill-health, isolation, and poverty. Children within these families are significantly more likely to be in trouble with the police and to be excluded from school (Lloyd et al., 2011).

• *Sure Start* is an area-based initiative, launched in 1998 in England (slightly different versions were developed in Wales, Scotland and Northern Ireland) and is now overseen by the Department for Education. Sure Start aimed to give 'children the best possible start in life' through the improvement of childcare, early education, and health and family support, with an emphasis on outreach and community development. *Every Child Matters* developed the Sure Start local programmes into Sure Start Children's Centres, controlled by local authorities and provided in every community, not just the most disadvantaged areas (DCSF, 2003). In 2012, the Coalition government replaced the Sure Start 'core offer', which set out a number of services that centres were required to provide, with a 'core purpose' to improve outcomes for young children and their parents, focusing particularly on families in greatest need. These changes have been introduced alongside a removal of the ring-fence for Sure Start funding and the first trials of payment-by-results measures (Department for Education, 2011).

The short-term nature of some intervention programmes, either due to legislative change or patterns of funding, has potentially limited their impact and effectiveness. Central funding for other intervention projects such as Positive Activities for Young People, Splash and Challenge and Support schemes ceased on 31 March 2013. Some of these projects secured sufficient funding from police and crime commissioners and other local partners to continue operating, but these schemes continue to be under threat from funding cuts and drives for efficiency (Pickford and Dugmore, 2012). There has been a lack of research and evaluation (especially long-term) of these programmes but that which has been conducted generally indicates that investment in early intervention and prevention schemes can successfully divert some young people from involvement in offending behaviour (Ross et al., 2011). As noted above, the number of first-time entrants to the youth justice system has decreased, despite concerns that **labelling** and **net-widening** through early intervention could draw more children and young people into the youth justice system.

As well as local and national schemes, children deemed at risk of becoming involved in anti-social or offending behaviour and their parents may be asked to enter into a voluntary contract or agreement, as a precursor to legal action.

- *Acceptable behaviour contracts* (ABCs) – a young person aged 10 and over who is involved in comparatively low-level anti-social behaviour may be asked to sign an ABC drawn up by the YOT. The contract is a voluntary agreement, whereby the young person (and his or her parents) agrees to stop the nuisance behaviour and to address the concerns of neighbours and the community. As a voluntary agreement, there is no penalty for not complying with the contract, but, in some instances, the failure to comply with an ABC has been used in support of an application for an anti-social behaviour order (ASBO).
- *Parenting contracts* are voluntary agreements between local agencies, such as schools or local education authorities, and a parent whose child is involved in offending behaviour, truancy or has been excluded from school. The contract sets out what parents must do to address the anti-social behaviour of their child and may contain conditions, such as making sure that a child goes to school regularly.

Civil legislation

Where intervention schemes or voluntary contracts are unavailable and/or ineffective in deterring a young person from involvement in offending behaviour, there are a range of legal sanctions and coercive measures also aimed at 'nipping in the bud' incipient offending or anti-social behaviour. Many of these are based on a 'zero tolerance' stance, and many are targeted towards children, arguably discriminating against them on the basis of their age and social status. Such civil measures include the following.

- *Child safety orders* (s. 11 CDA 1998) are a quasi-criminal, reactive measure that a local authority can apply for in the Family Court on the grounds that an act has been committed that would have been an offence had the child been aged 10 or over, or that a child has behaved in such a way as to suggest that they are at risk of offending or in such a way as to cause or be likely to cause disruption or harassment to local residents, or has breached a local child curfew order (see below). The purpose of a child safety order is to enforce supervision by a social worker or youth justice worker, normally for 3 months but possibly for up to 12 months. The court may impose any requirements deemed relevant to ensure that the child receives appropriate care, protection and support to prevent a repetition of the kind of behaviour that led to the order being made. If the child fails to comply with the requirements of the order, the court will have the option of considering care proceedings.
- *Local child curfews* (s. 14 CDA 1998, as amended by the Anti-Social Behaviour Act (ASBA) 2003) – if the district council concludes that there is a wider problem with the behaviour of children in general in the area, they can apply for a general local child curfew (not to be confused with individual curfew orders), which would have the effect of allowing the police to take a child home if found on the streets after certain hours stipulated in the orders. These orders can last up to 90 days and are renewable. Initially, the legislation applied to children aged under 10 but this was increased to under 16-year-olds by the ASBA 2003.
- *Dispersal orders* (ss 30–6 ASBA 2003) – where a police superintendent or above has reasonable grounds for believing that members of the public have been intimidated, harassed, alarmed or distressed in public places in a specific area and that anti-social behaviour is a significant and persistent problem in that area, they may, with the consent of the local authority, make a written authority for a dispersal order. This gives police officers and PCSOs the power to disperse groups of two or more young people and take home any young person under 16 who is out on the streets in a dispersal zone between 9pm and 6am and not accompanied by a parent or responsible adult (unless there are reasonable grounds for believing that they are likely to suffer significant harm

at home). The period of the order cannot exceed 6 months and the authorization notice must be either published in a local newspaper or conspicuously displayed in the relevant area before the period starts. Although a civil order, breach of a dispersal order is a criminal offence, punishable with a fine of up to £5000, up to 3 months' imprisonment, or both, which has implications for due process and other legal safeguards (discussed later). The Divisional Court found that the power for police to remove a child under s. 30 was permissive, not coercive (i.e. could not include any element of force) (*R (ex parte W) v Commissioner of the Police of the Metropolis* [2006]), but the Court of Appeal held that this measure 'plainly carries with it a coercive power' (*R (W) v (1) Commissioner of Police for the Metropolis (2) London Borough of Richmond-upon-Thames (3) Secretary of State for the Home Department* [2006]). The Court of Appeal went on to clarify that s. 30(6) 'does not confer an arbitrary power to remove children who are not involved in, nor at risk from exposure to, actual or imminently anticipated anti-social behaviour'. Legally, children are thus able to go to a dispersal zone without fear of being removed provided they do not participate in anti-social behaviour and that they avoid others who are behaving anti-socially, although how rigorously this is applied in practice is debatable.

- *Secure accommodation orders* (s. 25 Children Act 1989) – where a young person's physical or emotional state or offending or self-harming behaviour places them at risk of significant harm, and no other resource/provision is appropriate to reduce this risk, detention in secure accommodation may be considered. This may be by means of a secure accommodation order made by a court, or by means of the local authority exercising its power to restrict liberty without the consent of the court (the Children (Secure Accommodation) Regulations 1991). Local authorities may not keep a young person in secure accommodation without leave of the court beyond 72 hours (whether or not consecutive) in any period of 28 consecutive days, after which an application needs to be made to the Family Court. The court cannot make the order unless the child is legally represented in court. Children under 13 can only be kept in secure accommodation with the consent of the Secretary of State. The court can make a secure accommodation order for up to 3 months on the first application, and then for periods of up to 6 months on subsequent application. Regardless of the length of the court order, if, during the course of the order, the child no longer meets the criteria for an order, the local authority must remove the child from secure accommodation. The law provides for admissions into secure accommodation for three discrete groups of young people charged with criminal offences, discussed in later chapters: those who are detained by the police (Chapter 2); those who are remanded (Chapter 3); and those who are serving custodial sentences (Chapter 5).

• *Parenting orders* (various legislation) – where children are subject to child safety orders, ASBOs, IPNAs, or are convicted of an offence, the court may – and in some cases is compelled to – impose a parenting order, requiring parents to attend counselling guidance sessions for a period of 3–12 months, providing such sessions exist in their area (s. 8 CDA 1998). Parenting orders can also be issued if a young person is excluded from school (s. 20 ASBA 2003; s. 24 Police and Justice Act 2006) or fails to attend school (s. 41 Education and Skills Act 2008). Under ss 23–5 Police and Justice Act 2006, it is possible for local authorities and registered social landlords to enter into parenting contracts and apply for parenting orders. Conditions of the order may include attending school meetings, requiring the parent to ensure their child is at home at particular times, or that they do not visit certain places unsupervised. An assessment of parenting circumstances is essential in enabling the court to make a judgment on whether to pass a parenting order, so should be included in a PSR (Chapter 3), or a SAF assessment. Failure to comply with a parenting order can result in a maximum fine of £1000.

Anti-social behaviour

Anti-social behaviour is a contentious, relatively new concept in terms of police activity, legal responses, public expectations and political aspirations. Such unwanted, nuisance behaviour has clearly always existed but was managed outside the civil and criminal justice systems. It was only when New Labour announced its 'Tough on Crime, Tough on the Causes of Crime' campaign in the build-up to the 1997 general election that it became a specific target for intervention. However, it is not at all clear what 'anti-social behaviour' actually is, nor where the boundary between criminal behaviour and anti-social behaviour lies (Johns, 2011). The CDA 1998 defined anti-social behaviour as: 'Acting in a manner that caused or was likely to cause harassment, alarm or distress to one or more persons not of the same household as (the defendant)' – a broad and ill-defined area of behaviour. Arguably, there has been a decrease in tolerance for this kind of behaviour and people are more likely to turn to sources of authority and demand government action than draw on their own resources and informal networks to maintain social order, as perhaps previously occurred. Much anti-social behaviour is seen to be committed mainly by children and young people, but there is considerable debate as to whether anti-social behaviour is just adolescent 'silliness', a transgression of socially desirable behaviour, or actual criminality (Fox and Arnull, 2013). If anti-social behaviour is just adolescent 'naughtiness', formal intervention could exacerbate the situation by unnecessarily drawing an individual into the criminal justice system. Where the behaviour is more clearly criminal, it could, and perhaps should, be managed through existing criminal sanctions.

Injunctions to prevent nuisance and annoyance

ASBOs, introduced by the CDA 1998, have been extensively criticized for needlessly criminalizing and stigmatizing individuals and groups within society (such as children, those from minority ethnic backgrounds and those with mental health problems or learning disabilities), being discriminatory towards children and young people, and failing to prevent anti-social behaviour. Despite this, the Coalition government replaced the ASBO (and the associated anti-social behaviour injunctions and individual support orders) with the IPNA in the Anti-Social Behaviour, Crime and Policing Act 2014. These are preventative orders; rather than punishing previous behaviour, the orders place restrictions (such as curfews, geographical and association restrictions) on an individual with the aim of preventing further anti-social behaviour. Anti-social behaviour, in this guise, is treated as a civil offence and requires only proof on the balance of probabilities rather than the criminal **standard of proof** – disregarding *R v Manchester Crown Court, ex parte McCann and Others* [2002] that held that the imposition of an ASBO should be decided on the criminal standard of being beyond reasonable doubt. Designating the process of obtaining an IPNA as a civil procedure means that the traditional due process protections associated with criminal proceedings are circumvented. This increases the risk that the sanctions applied may be disproportionate to the harm caused (Brown, 2013) and that the conditions of an IPNA may be more wide-reaching and last longer than the penalties for a similar offence dealt with under existing criminal law. The Court of Appeal held that ASBOs should not impose prohibitions so numerous that they make compliance difficult (for example, *Boness, Bebbington and Others* [2006]) and it may be assumed that IPNAs will be expected to conform similarly, but this is yet to be seen.

IPNAs can be issued by a court to anyone aged 10 or above on the application by a relevant agency, including the police, British Transport Police, local authorities, registered social landlords/housing associations, NHS Protect, Transport for London and the Environment Agency. The maximum term for children and young people is 12 months; as well as prohibitions aimed at preventing anti-social behaviour, the court can also include positive requirements intended to address the underlying reasons for the young person's behaviour. The Coalition attempted to broaden the definition of anti-social behaviour that could trigger an IPNA, but this was rejected in the House of Lords and the definition remains as it was in the CDA 1998: 'conduct that has caused, or is likely to cause, harassment, alarm or distress to any person' (Anti-Social Behaviour, Crime and Policing Act 2014).

The court can apply a power of arrest against any prohibition or requirement, apart from the requirement to participate in particular activities; a police officer may arrest without warrant an individual who is reasonably suspected to be in breach of that prohibition or requirement. While breach of an ASBO was considered to be a criminal offence, breach of an IPNA is treated as contempt of court; the court retains its inherent contempt of court sentencing powers (for example, no further action to be taken or issuing a fine) but, in addition, was given two specific powers in Schedule 5A Policing and Crime Act 2009.

- *Civil supervision order* – YOTs are required to supervise young people for up to 6 months; the order contains a supervision requirement and/or an activity requirement, and/or a curfew requirement. A supervision requirement requires the young person to attend appointments with a responsible officer of the YOT at a particular time and place, as specified. An activity requirement may be made requiring the young person to participate in a particular activity or residential activity for a specified number of days (not fewer than 12 or more than 24). A residential activity requirement may last for a period of not more than 7 days, and the young person's parent/carer needs to give permission. A curfew requirement places an obligation on the young person to remain in a particular place for specified periods (not less than 2 hours and not more than 8 hours on any given day); an electronic monitoring requirement to enforce compliance with the terms of the curfew can be ordered. It is the responsibility of the YOT officer to ensure that any necessary arrangements are made to enable the young person's compliance with the order and to promote their compliance. The young person is responsible for keeping in touch with the responsible officer and for notifying any change of address. At the time of writing, there are no national standards governing the administration of these orders.

- *Civil detention order* – where a young person has been found to have breached a civil supervision order, the court may revoke that order and either make a new supervision order (possibly with more stringent conditions) or make a civil detention order. The court can use its discretion and impose a detention order purely as a punishment for contempt, or as a means of mitigating serious concerns about the young person's safety or the risk they pose to others; the court must consider a report prepared by the YOT for that purpose. A civil detention order may last for no more than 3 months (beginning on the day the order is made). The young person may be detained in local authority secure accommodation, a secure training centre (STC), or a young offender institution. Unlike **detention and training orders** (DTOs), civil detention orders do not contain a post-custody licence period and there is no statutory obligation for post-release supervision, but it is likely that the young person will need support when they are released from custody. This could be provided through the existing requirements and prohibitions of the prior injunction, or the court can be requested to vary the requirements or prohibitions, to ensure they are appropriate and supportive.

These powers are at odds with other civil orders, as children cannot usually be detained for civil contempt of court. They also risk providing a disproportionate response to children's behaviour, particularly when it is recognized that many children breach the conditions of their orders due to an inability to understand, or understand how to comply with, the prohibitions of their order, rather than wilful non-compliance (Children's Society et al., 2013). A civil detention order is essentially a sentence of imprisonment for a child or young person, as they are held in the same institutions as those serving detention and training orders or other custodial sentences, and it has the same concomitant risks (see Chapter 5).

Criminal behaviour order

In addition to replacing ASBOs, the Anti-Social Behaviour, Crime and Policing Act 2014 replaced ASBOs on conviction (also known as CRASBOs) with the criminal behaviour order (CBO). A CBO can be applied for by the prosecutor on conviction for any criminal offence and can be made against a child or young person if the court is satisfied, beyond reasonable doubt, that the individual has engaged in behaviour that caused, or was likely to cause, harassment, alarm or distress, and that it considers that making the order will help prevent a recurrence of such behaviour. Again, due process safeguards are removed in that the CBO may relate to wider behaviour than that proved through the criminal conviction and hearsay evidence is allowed in CBO proceedings; furthermore the automatic reporting restrictions that normally apply in legal proceedings for children and young people under the CYPA 1933 are lifted in CBO hearings. Breach of a CBO is a criminal offence; breach proceedings are held in the Youth Court meaning that the maximum sentence available is a 2-year detention and training order (DTO).

Gang injunctions

The Policing and Crime Act 2009 contained provision for civil injunctions to prevent gang-related violence to be sought against an individual aged over 18. Since January 2012, the police and local authorities have been able to apply to a County Court for a gang injunction against a young person aged between 14 and 17, under the Crime and Security Act 2010. Similarly to IPNAs, gang injunctions are civil orders and the civil standard of proof on the balance of probability is sufficient for an injunction to be passed. The police or local authority applying for the injunction must have evidence that the respondent either has engaged in, encouraged, or assisted gang-related violence, or is about to do so. The court must believe that a gang injunction is necessary to prevent the young person from being involved in gang-related violence and/or to protect them from such violence (MoJ/YJB, undated/a). Between January 2012 and January 2014, only two of the 88 gang injunctions awarded related to under-18s, perhaps due to a lack of awareness and understanding of gang injunctions among police officers, local authorities, legal representatives and the judiciary, as well as some uncertainty about the benefits of gang injunctions compared with other interventions. However, the Home Office has expressed a desire to increase the use of injunctions and the power to issue gang injunctions for under-18s has been moved from the civil courts to Youth Courts (Crime and Courts Act 2013).

Definitions of the term 'gang' vary, but the Policing and Crime Act 2009 defines gang-related violence as violence or a threat of violence that occurs in the course of, or is otherwise related to, the activities of a group that:

- consists of at least three people;
- uses a name, emblem or colour or has any other characteristic that enables its members to be identified by others as a group; and
- is associated with a particular area.

The injunction should specify reasonable prohibitions or requirements that the young person must adhere to. As with IPNAs, the court can apply a power of arrest against any prohibition, or any requirement, apart from the requirement to participate in particular activities; a police officer may arrest without warrant an individual who is reasonably suspected to be in breach of that prohibition or requirement. Failure to

---

▸ PRACTICE FOCUS

Residents have complained to their PCSO that members of a local family have been involved in anti-social behaviour and causing distress to the community. In particular, two of the younger children, aged 9 and 8, have been seen engaging in acts of vandalism, such as damaging garden gates and fences, throwing stones at cars and breaking flower pots and garden statues. Two older children, aged 11 and 13, have been verbally abusive to residents, threatening them with physical harm and shouting racist abuse, although no direct physical harm has been caused.

- What factors would need to be considered if an assessment of these children is requested?
- What proceedings could the PCSO initiate in respect of the two younger children?
- What interventions might be proposed for the two older children?

comply with the specified terms of an injunction can result in breach proceedings and is dealt with as a civil contempt of court, with the court being able to take no further action, issue a fine, or make a civil supervision order or a civil detention order (see above).

Discrimination and rights

Arguably, the criminal justice system and elements of wider society discriminate against children as a group within society. As noted in the Introduction, the UN Committee on the Rights of the Child (2008; see also CRAE, 2013) has expressed concern at the UK's intolerance and negativity towards children and young people, in particular, recommending the abolition of ASBOs, ending the use of 'mosquitos' (a high-frequency sound emitted to stop children gathering in groups outside shops, which cannot be heard by adults and therefore directly discriminates against children on purely aged-based criteria), and raising the age of criminal responsibility in line with international recommendations. Much of the media, particularly the tabloid press, has exacerbated the discrimination children and young people experience by drawing sweeping generalizations and encouraging a '**moral panic**' about youth crime (Cohen, 1972; Jenks 1996), which in turn fuels punitive reactions towards young people and furthers the public's fear of them.

More specifically, s. 95 Criminal Justice Act 1991 refers to a duty of those involved in the criminal justice system to avoid discrimination against anyone 'on the ground of race or sex or any other improper ground' and professionals are required to act fairly in relation to race (Equality Act 2010). Nonetheless, as noted above, gender and racial discrimination is apparent within much of the youth justice system, including responses from the police and courts. There is also evidence of discrimination against children with disabilities, mental health problems (Prison Reform Trust, 2010; Prison Reform Trust and Young Minds, 2013), and traveller and gypsy children (Cemlyn et al., 2009). Some discrimination may be the unintended consequences of legislation and policy, in other instances it may be the result of systematic discrimination (Goldson and Muncie, 2006). The intersectionality of racism, class and gender can exacerbate the experience of discrimination, but the youth justice system arguably does not address multiple oppressions and often compounds rather than alleviates them (Bates and Swan, 2014).

Managing anti-social behaviour and diverting young people from the criminal justice system are clearly important activities, reducing the negative impact of harmful or distressing behaviour on victims and improving the life chances of young people who might otherwise be drawn further into the youth justice system. However, such interventions may have far-reaching and oppressive consequences (Fox and Arnull, 2013). Those subject to increased surveillance and enforcement, through civil or criminal legislation, tend to be those who are already socially marginalized, experiencing disadvantage and/or poverty. Indeed, some intervention programmes may potentially increase the disempowerment, disenfranchisement and marginalization of young people (Fox and Arnull, 2013). For example, families already disadvantaged by health, educational or social problems may struggle to control, let alone change, a child's behaviour; in some instances, parents may be held accountable for the behaviour of their children to the extent of being fined or even evicted, with the concomitant negative impacts on the whole family.

Civil measures, such as dispersal orders, IPNAs and gang injunctions (as well as other civil penalties noted in Chapter 4) potentially breach children's rights by bypassing the due process protections of the criminal justice system and effectively providing for a criminal penalty equivalent to a community sentence for a person alleged, but not proven to the criminal standard, to have been involved in anti-social behaviour or gang-related violence. It is questionable whether a civil standard of proof can be considered as 'convincing' evidence that a child is involved in offending or anti-social behaviour. Concerns may also arise where children and young people have believed themselves to be under pressure to acknowledge their involvement in an incident and/or give consent for their involvement in early intervention or diversionary programmes, as research suggests that children are more likely to make false admissions of guilt (see Chapter 2). Further, the UNCRC stipulates that any acknowledgment of guilt or involvement will not be used again a child or young person in any subsequent legal proceedings, but failure to comply with the requirements of early intervention measures, such as ABCs, has been given as evidence in support of applications for ASBOs and legal proceedings against families at risk of eviction (Fair Play for Children, 2011).

Early intervention and prevention programmes have an implicit risk of **deviancy amplification** and labelling (Becker, 1963; Cohen, 1972); increased police surveillance and more intensive responses can amplify the problems some young people face and exacerbate difficulties with relationships within the community (Waiton, 2001). Unless positively managed, children may feel ashamed or embarrassed by their involvement in diversionary programmes, which can lead to feelings of increased isolation and social exclusion, rather than social reintegration. There remains an overarching question of whether legal responses, such as IPNAs, curfews and dispersal orders, can increase the division between some adults and children, by enhancing feelings of fear and anxiety (Waiton, 2001; Wain with Burney, 2007). Many early intervention and prevention programmes risk breaching the rights of children under the UNCRC 1989 and the Human Rights Act 1998. For example, children receiving ASBOs/IPNAs do not have the right to anonymity that would be granted to them within the Youth Court – children may be publicly identified and exposed to a negative public reaction, including the risk of physical harm, raising child protection concerns and potentially hampering their rehabilitation (Hart, 2014; see also Chapter 6). Dispersal orders, IPNAs and gang injunctions can deprive children of their right to freedom of association and place unfair restrictions on their liberty.

Conclusions

The remit of the youth justice system, and those working within it, has expanded considerably to encompass a focus on diversion, prevention and early intervention. Some of these measures are voluntary, others are quasi-legal or involve civil legislation. While many can lead to positive outcomes for children and young people on the fringes of offending behaviour, and can offer victims and communities some respite from perceived anti-social behaviour, there are concerns that the lowering of the standard of proof required and the increasing sanctions for alleged anti-social behaviour may have an adverse impact on some children and young people. The number of first-time entrants into the youth justice system has decreased significantly but the fear of and antipathy towards children, many of whom are assumed to be involved in offending or anti-social behaviour, remains high. Policy-makers need to make certain that developments in policy and legislation do not serve to increase fear levels towards children and young people, in particular those who are involved in offending behaviour, such that children and young people's rights are upheld, their identities protected and they are enabled to benefit from the positive early intervention and prevention programmes that youth justice agencies may offer. The increasing emphasis on risk assessment and risk management within both practice and policy warrants consideration, with practitioners needing to reflect on their practice to ensure that assessments and interventions are holistic, non-discriminatory and promote inclusion. The following chapter explores the legislation surrounding children and young people's contact with the police, highlighting the need to balance the demands of the youth justice process with the welfare of the child and his or her specific rights.

Further reading

Baker K, G Kelly and B Wilkinson (2011) *Assessment in Youth Justice* provides a detailed consideration of the assessment process within the youth justice system.

Farrington, D P and B C Welsh (2007*) Saving Children from a Life of Crime: Early Risk Factors and Effective Interventions* considers the research evidence for risk assessments and prevention and early intervention programmes.

Newburn, T (2013) *Criminology* provides an accessible, comprehensive overview of criminological theories that attempt to explain the causes of offending behaviour.

Wain N with Burney E (2007) *The ASBO: Wrong Turning, Dead End*; and

Waiton, S (2001) *Scared of the Kids*? *Curfews, Crime and the Regulation of Young People* – both of these books explore the criminalization of children and young people through the administration of crime prevention measures (specifically ASBOs and curfews) and the potential harm to social and community relationships that can result. All the authors argue that such measures can lead to an increased fear of crime felt by adults and the social alienation of children and young people.

2
ARREST AND DETENTION BY THE POLICE

AT A GLANCE THIS CHAPTER COVERS:

- stop and search
- police powers of arrest
- at the police station
- appropriate adults
- achieving best evidence
- decision to charge
- youth restorative disposals
- youth cautions and youth conditional cautions
- charge and prosecution
- police bail

This chapter discusses the legal processes involved when children and young people are stopped and searched by the police, arrested and/or detained in a police station, with reference to the Police and Criminal Evidence Act (PACE) 1984 and associated legislation and guidance. Particular attention is given to the role of **appropriate adults** and guidance relating to interviewing and detaining children and young people in the police station. Tensions between processes in the police station and the UNCRC are considered, for example, the limitation of the right to silence, as an illustration of children and young people's particular vulnerabilities within the youth justice system. Issues of discrimination and inequality are discussed, for example, ethnic and racial discrimination within police stop and search practice. The range of powers available to the police in regard to children and young people is discussed, including **youth cautions** and **youth conditional cautions** (YCCs), and **youth restorative disposals** (YRDs).

Stop and search

Under s. 1 PACE 1984, the police have the power to stop and search any person (including children and young people) or vehicle for stolen or prohibited articles (Code A, Annex A); they are also granted extensive powers to stop and search under other laws. The procedures surrounding a stop and search are clearly regulated in policy, although the extent to which these regulations are upheld is arguable. Before a search, police officers should give their name and the reason for the search; after the search, police officers should make a proper record including a note of the person's ethnic origin; intimate searches (more than a search of outer clothes) must take place away from public view and should be carried out by a police officer of the same sex; the stop and search must be brief and the search must take place at or near the place of the stop (Code A). Reasonable force may be used to conduct the search if co-operation is refused, but only as a last resort.

There is an expectation that the powers will be used fairly, responsibly, respectfully and without unlawful discrimination: an individual should not be searched without reasonable grounds for doing so, even if the person consents to it; personal factors (age, race, appearance, known previous convictions, religion) alone are not reasonable grounds for suspicion that a stop and search is warranted. However, there is comprehensive evidence to suggest that discrimination, both on an individual and an institutional level, is prevalent within stop and search practice, with black and Asian people being significantly more likely to be stopped and searched than white people (Equality and Human Rights Commission, 2010). Medina-Ariza (2014) found that police were more likely to stop and search a young person on grounds of a young person's ethnicity, whom they associated with, and a focus on 'the usual suspects', rather than the particular behaviour of the young person.

On-the-spot questions	1 What factors might lead to racial discrimination within police stop and search practice?
	2 How can such discrimination be reduced?

Police powers of arrest

If the police have reasonable grounds to believe that an offence has been committed, they may arrest a child or young person aged over 10. Although the child will usually be taken to the police station, a police officer can grant bail anywhere (known as 'street bail'), under s. 4 Criminal Justice Act (CJA) 2003, requiring the child to attend a designated police station at a later date.

The Serious Organised Crime and Police Act (SOCPA) 2005 removed the division between arrestable and non-arrestable offences that existed under PACE 1984 and police have the power to make an arrest for any criminal offence, no matter how trivial, if the police officer has reasonable grounds to believe that a person is committing, has committed or is about to commit an offence and, importantly, that an arrest is necessary for any of the criteria listed in s. 110(5) SOCPA 2005:

s. 110(5)

    (a) to enable the name of the person in question to be ascertained (in the case where the constable does not know, and cannot readily ascertain, the person's name, or has reasonable grounds for doubting whether a name given by the person as his name is his real name);

    (b) correspondingly as regards the person's address;

    (c) to prevent the person in question—

        (i) causing physical injury to himself or any other person;

        (ii) suffering physical injury;

       (iii) causing loss of or damage to property;

       (iv) committing an offence against public decency (subject to subsection (6)); or

       (v) causing an unlawful obstruction of the highway;

  (d) to protect a child or other vulnerable person from the person in question;

  (e) to allow the prompt and effective investigation of the offence or of the conduct of the person in question;

  (f) to prevent any prosecution for the offence from being hindered by the disappearance of the person in question.

(6) Subsection (5)(c)(iv) applies only where members of the public going about their normal business cannot reasonably be expected to avoid the person in question.

Arrest remains discretionary and police officers should consider whether their objectives can be met using less intrusive means (Code G, PACE 1984 Codes of Practice), including taking no further action, an out-of-court disposal (discussed below), or informing the individual that they will be 'reported', with the officer submitting a report for the question of prosecution to be considered by the police and Crown Prosecution Service (CPS). If the case is referred to the CPS, it may decide to prosecute the offender and arrange for a summons to attend court to be served or take no further action.

The power to arrest for a breach of the peace is unaffected by SOCPA 2005 because it is not deemed a criminal offence within the context of PACE 1984. Accordingly, the provisions of PACE 1984 do not apply to arrest and detention for causing a breach of the peace (*Williamson v Chief Constable of the West Midlands Police* [2003]). The police thus have the power to arrest anyone for breach of the peace (either occurring in public or in private) and whenever harm is done, or is likely to be done, to a person, in his or her presence, or to his or her property; or a person is genuinely in fear of being harmed through an assault, affray, riot, unlawful assembly, or disturbance. The police can use this power to stop a fight and also to arrest someone and hold on to the individual until after the fight. The arrested person can only expect to be released after the risk of the breach restarting has passed. Common law also allows any person to arrest someone if they are committing, or about to commit, a breach of the peace.

In addition, the police have the power under s. 136 PACE 1984 to detain an individual whom they suspect is mentally unwell even if no offence has been committed. Concerns were raised by the Care Quality Commission (2014) that police cells are being inappropriately used as a 'default place of safety' for children and young people experiencing a severe mental health episode due to a lack of age-appropriate mental health facilities. The government responded by issuing a *Mental Health Crisis Care Concordat* (Department of Health, 2014), which states that local areas should establish protocols for dealing with children and young people detained under the Act and ensure police custody is never used as a place of safety for children and young people except in exceptional circumstances. In such cases, the use of cells should be avoided and alternatives within the police station should be considered.

As with stop and search powers, there is evidence of discrimination with arrest rates, with more black and Asian people being arrested than white (Ashworth and Redmayne, 2010). The use of force, including discharging tasers, against children and young people during arrest also warrants monitoring. In response to a parliamentary question asked by Liberal Democrat backbencher Julian Huppert, figures showed armed officers discharged, targeted or threatened to use tasers against children and young people more than 320 times in 2011 – an 11-fold increase from 2007, when they were authorized for use against under-18s in England. There are particular concerns about the use of force, including the use of tasers, for children who have learning disabilities, mental health problems, emotional or behavioural difficulties.

At the police station

When a child is arrested and taken to the police station, he or she has an unqualified right (under PACE 1984) to have a friend, relative or other person told of their arrest and detention at the station. Children and young people aged 10–16 also have the right to have an independent 'appropriate adult' present during questioning and other custody procedures (s. 66 PACE 1984, as amended by SOCPA 2005). The situation for 17-year-olds is more complex (see key case analysis); despite the UNCRC stating that all those aged under 18 should be considered as children, youth justice legislation is inconsistent and only slowly being brought into line with such international agreements.

R (on the Application of HC) v Secretary of State for the Home Department and Commissioner of Police for the Metropolis [2013]: treating 17-year-olds as adult and providing appropriate adults

Approximately 75,000 17-year-olds are taken into police custody each year. Until recently they were treated as adults, despite both the Children Act 1989 and the UNCRC stating that all those under 18 are children. Specifically, the provision of an appropriate adult was not a right for 17-year-olds, which was challenged in *R (on the Application of HC) v Secretary of State for the Home Department and Commissioner of Police for the Metropolis* [2013].

Hughes Cousins-Chang was arrested 4 weeks after his 17th birthday on suspicion of the robbery of a mobile phone on a bus, but no adult was informed of his arrest for more than 4 hours, after his request to contact his mother was refused by the police. He was held in police custody for 12 hours and was subject to a strip-search. A month later, he was informed that his bail would be cancelled and no charge was laid. He challenged the legality of treating 17-year-olds as adults under the ECHR.

A High Court judgment in April 2013 held that the practice of treating 17-year-olds as adults, the failure to inform parents of their child's arrest and the failure to provide an appropriate adult to 17-year-old children was in breach of Article 8 ECHR; the interpretation of which must be informed by the UNCRC and associated national laws such as the Children Acts 1989 and 2004, which establish the age of majority as 18.

The judgment concluded that:

> … it is inconsistent with the rights of the claimant and his mother, enshrined in Article 8 [ECHR], for the Secretary of State to treat 17 year-olds as adults when in detention. To do so disregards the definition of a child in the UNCRC, in all the other international instruments to which the Strasbourg Court and the Supreme Court have referred, and the preponderance of legislation affecting children and justice which include within their scope those who are under 18. The Secretary of State's failure to amend Code C is in breach of her obligation under the Human Rights Act 1998, and unlawful. (para. 89)

The Association of Chief Police Officers has advised all forces that they should offer appropriate adults to 17-year-olds, but other safeguards for 17-year-olds have not been implemented such that they are not given the same consideration as those aged 16 and under. The government's proposals have been criticized for failing to reflect the spirit of the decision – that all under-18s should be accorded the rights afforded to children when at the police station, including the right to be transferred to the care of a local authority, rather than detained in a police cell (CRAE, 2013).

On-the-spot questions	1 Why should 17-year-olds be treated as children by the youth justice system?
	2 What are the implications for practice of treating 17-year-olds as children within the police station?

The appropriate adult

The role of the appropriate adult aims to help safeguard the rights and civil liberties of the child, ensuring that they can understand the police proceedings; their main focus should be on the physical and emotional well-being of the child, rather than whether or not the young person has committed an offence (Children's Legal Centre, undated). It is the solicitor's role to advise a young person as to process issues, the evidence against them, their plea and issues of bail. If the child does not wish to have a solicitor present, the appropriate adult may instruct a solicitor at any time on behalf of the child, or instruct a solicitor to advise him or her as an appropriate adult. A child has the right to consult with a lawyer in the absence of the appropriate adult if they wish.

When a child is detained, the custody officer must identify the person responsible for the child's welfare, inform them that the child has been arrested, the reasons why, and where the child is being detained, and ask them to attend the police station to see the child. The choice of who will act as the appropriate adult initially lies with the child and can be:

- a parent or guardian – unless they are suspected of involvement in the offence, are the victim, a witness, or are otherwise involved in the investigation; or
- a duty social worker or member of the local YOT; or
- another responsible adult aged 18 or over who is not a police officer, employed by the police or present at the police station in a professional

capacity (for example, a solicitor), such as a youth worker whom the child knows or a relative (including a sibling).

The YOT has an obligation to coordinate the appropriate adult service under s. 39 CDA 1998; this provision varies, with schemes using volunteers and/or YOT workers, or commercial providers (HM Inspectorate of Constabulary et al., 2011). There is some ambiguity in the role and there was limited guidance for YOTs in making initial arrangements for appropriate adult services (Pierpoint, 2004). The appropriate adult plays an important part in providing continuity for children and young people, who may have contact with a range of different officers and staff while they are in police custody (HM Inspectorate of Constabulary et al., 2011).

The potential for a conflict of roles arises for social workers acting as appropriate adults: both the British Association of Social Workers and the Association of Directors of Children's Services believe that social workers have a duty to assist in the prevention and detection of crime and that, if asked, should pass on relevant information to the police. Thus, a social worker who is party to information divulged during an interview may feel obliged to pass the information to the police yet also want to support the young person (Children's Legal Centre, undated). For example, if a looked after child admits an offence to their social worker, but is not prepared to admit it to the police, it would be advisable for an alternative appropriate adult to be appointed.

The appropriate adult has particular responsibilities, for example, being required to be present when the young person is told of their rights and entitlements, when they are interviewed and when they are charged (HM Inspectorate of Constabulary et al., 2011), and in recording details of the process (for example, noting the place of detention, time of and grounds for arrest, name and rank of the arresting officer and custody officer, and time they were informed of the child's arrest). However, it appears that the appropriate adult provision has moved from a position of safeguarding and promoting the welfare of the child to a focus on complying with PACE 1984. For example, an inadequate information flow between YOTs and appropriate adults has led to the latter being ill-prepared to take a proactive role in promoting the needs of the child, which could be exacerbated by incorrect or incomplete custody records; and some appropriate adults have been seen to be passive and unlikely to challenge the police (HM Inspectorate of Constabulary et al., 2011). The National Appropriate Adult Network (see further reading, below) provides more detailed guidance and information on the role of the appropriate adult.

Legal advice

The right to legal advice is guaranteed by s. 58 PACE 1984; such advice was originally provided through a system of duty solicitors within the police station. However, pressure to reduce spending on legal aid has led to requests being made to the Defence Solicitor Call Centre which will either attempt to contact a nominated solicitor or the duty solicitor, or to forward the request to a telephone advice centre. Concerns have been raised about the quality of legal representation for children and young people (Independent Parliamentarians' Inquiry, 2014; see Chapter 4). In particular, there is often inadequate access to telephones in police stations, resulting in a lack of privacy (Ashworth and Redmayne, 2010), and there are potential difficulties for children and young people receiving advice via the telephone (for example, in communicating, understanding or remembering the advice given) and the quality of advice given via telephone is debatable (Hucklesby, 2013).

Voluntary attendance at a police station

Any individual, including children and young people, may be asked to attend the police station voluntarily for the purpose of assisting the police with an investigation – to clear up misunderstandings or provide further information relating to an offence – and may subsequently be arrested. The police cannot compel anyone to be a volunteer and anyone who attends voluntarily is free to leave the police station at any time. A young person aged under 18 must be accompanied by an appropriate adult and both are entitled to free and independent legal advice whilst in the station. A lack of cooperation may result in an arrest and the authorization of further detention for questioning.

Although the PACE 1984 Codes of Practice state that a child attending voluntarily at the station should not be treated with any less consideration than an arrested child, much of the protection given under PACE 1984 and its Codes does not apply to a volunteer. For example:

- there is no limit on the period of time a volunteer may remain at the station;
- the volunteer (and appropriate adult) need not be informed of the existence of the Codes of Practice; and

- unless cautioned, the volunteer (and appropriate adult) need not to be told of the right to communicate freely with the outside world or to consult privately with a solicitor.

These are unqualified rights, but are exercisable only on request.

The police interview

Police interviews with children and young people are subject to PACE 1984 and the Codes of Practice, recognizing that:

> Although juveniles … are often capable of providing reliable evidence, they may without knowing or wishing to do so, be particularly prone in certain circumstances to provide information which is unreliable, misleading or self-incriminating. Special care should therefore always be exercised in questioning such a person.
>
> *Code C, Notes for Guidance:11B*

The vast majority of police interviews are recorded (either by video and/or audio equipment); exceptionally they may be written down (Children's Legal Centre, undated). The interview recording forms part of the evidence against the child and a copy of the recording can be obtained by the legal representative, appropriate adult or the child if the child is charged or if a complaint is to be made about the conduct of the police. The interviewing officer should explain the appropriate adult's role in the interview, which is not to simply act as an observer but to advise the young person as to their rights (although not to provide legal advice about their plea), to observe whether or not the interview is being conducted properly and fairly, and to facilitate communication, for example, intervening to prevent the use of confusing, intimidating or leading questions. Any offensive or racist remarks or incidences of potential oppression and bullying should be noted by the appropriate adult who can then raise any concerns with the young person's parents/guardians and/or solicitor.

The child must be cautioned about their right to silence before any questions about their suspected involvement in an offence are put – the police caution is relatively complex and there are considerable doubts about how well it is understood (Ashworth and Redmayne, 2010). It is of particular concern for children and young people that the right to silence is no longer a complete right: prior to the Criminal Justice and Public Order Act (CJPOA) 1994 a suspect could choose to say nothing in a police interview and the right could not be questioned by the courts. A significant change (s. 34 CJPOA 1994) means a court may now be invited to draw an adverse inference from a detainee's refusal to answer questions in the police interview, so it is arguably rarely in their best interests to remain silent. The caution given is:

> You do not have to say anything, but it may harm your defence if you do not mention when questioned something which you later rely on in court. Anything you do say may be given in evidence.

Children and young people are over-represented in the number of false confessions made for a number of reasons, including the socialization of children and young people to respect authority and to want to please (Drizin and Leo, 2004; Bates and Swan, 2014). Children are particularly suggestible (Gudjonsson et al., 2009) and there are concerns that some appropriate adults may inadvertently pressure children into making false admissions of guilt. Children may also be less aware of the consequences of a false confession and may admit to involvement in offences so that they can be released from the police station, without considering the longer-term implications of their admission. As such, the removal of the complete right to silence is particularly detrimental to children and young people.

The CJPOA 1994 also introduced a 'special warning' which may be given by an interviewing officer when a child or young person fails or refuses to account for objects or substances found in their possession or at the place or time of the arrest.

The interview should be concluded as soon as the interviewing officer is satisfied that sufficient information to make a decision as to case disposal has been obtained and after the child and appropriate adult have been given the opportunity to make any further comments. The child has the right to also make a formal written statement if they so wish, and should take legal advice on this. If a child or young person is subsequently charged with an offence, further interviews should only be conducted if new evidence comes to light or where the police want to alert the young person to the content of a written statement or interview with another person. The child has the right for an appropriate adult and a solicitor to be present at any further interviews.

Achieving Best Evidence interviews

Interview practice during questioning by the police and in court (Chapter 3) should be guided by the principles of *Achieving Best Evidence*

(MoJ, 2011). It is of note, however, that this guidance was written for inter-views with victims and vulnerable witnesses and, under s. 19(1)(a) Youth Justice and Criminal Evidence Act (YJCE) 1999, child defendants were specif-ically excluded from the **special measures** provisions. While child victims and witnesses are deemed vulnerable by reason of age (s. 16 YJCE 1999, as amended by the Coroners and Justice Act 2009), child defendants are seen to be given sufficient protection by their solicitor or the duty solicitor and are not eligible for further measures. This discrepancy in treatment is even more apparent when the additional mental health or communication diffi-culties of many children who offend are considered (Talbot, 2012). Some concessions to young defendants have been made, particularly in relation to the court process, but there is a lack of equality in relation to the meas-ures that are available for young victims and witnesses and those available for young defendants (CRAE, 2013). This is discussed further in Chapter 3.

Taking photographs, fingerprints and other biometric data

Children and young people arrested and taken to a police station may be requested to have their fingerprints or photographs taken. When the child is under 14, consent to taking photographs, fingerprints and body samples must be given by a parent or guardian. Between the ages of 14 and 16, consent must be given by the child and the appropriate adult. It is not yet certain what the position for young people aged 17 will be (see key case analysis). Under the Codes of Practice, there are a number of situations where fingerprints may be taken without consent, for exam-ple: where there are reasonable grounds for suspecting that the finger-print evidence will tend to confirm or disprove any involvement in an offence; or to establish identity where the young person has refused to identify him or herself; or the police have reasonable grounds to suspect that they are not who they claim to be.

Children and young people may also be required to give samples – the need for the presence of an appropriate adult and for consent differs for intimate and non-intimate samples. A court may draw adverse infer-ences if consent is withheld by a child or young person (and/or their parent, where necessary) without good cause. Samples may be taken to establish whether a young person aged over 14 has used specified Class A drugs, such as heroin or cocaine (s. 63b PACE 1984), if they have been charged with a 'trigger' offence, which police have reasonable grounds for believing was caused by, or contributed to their drug use. Failure to provide a sample is an offence.

There has been considerable debate about the legality and appropriateness of retaining the biometric records, including fingerprints and DNA profiles, of individuals arrested but not charged or charged but acquitted, on police databases, particularly for children and young people (Campbell and Lynch, 2012). The Court of Appeal held that this does not contravene either Article 8 or Article 14 ECHR but an appeal to the House of Lords led to some safeguards being implemented under the Protection of Freedoms Act 2012. The Act stipulates that data from those arrested but not charged or acquitted of a minor offence should not be retained and existing records will be removed and samples destroyed. Furthermore, the Act states that the profiles of children convicted of a single minor offence should also be deleted/not retained, but this has not yet been fully implemented.

Identification parades

Children and young people may consent to being involved in an identification parade, which is usually a 'virtual' video parade. If the young person refuses to consent to participation, group identification may be utilized, whereby a victim or witness may be invited to identify the individual from part of an informal group, such as among people in a station or shopping centre, or in a closed circuit television image. Withholding consent can be given in evidence at any subsequent trial.

Searches

A child or young person may be searched at the time of initial detention or during detention, including a strip search if there is a reasonable suspicion of concealment. The appropriate adult should be present for a strip search (involving the removal of more than outer clothing), unless the young person informs the police that they do not want them there. A police officer should only be authorized to carry out the search as a last resort and must be of the same sex as the young person. An exception to these rules may be made if it is necessary to act quickly in an emergency.

An intimate search (of a person's bodily orifices, other than their mouth) may be carried out if the police have reasonable grounds for believing that the child has concealed either an article that may cause physical injury to him or herself or to others or a Class A drug, or to look for any items that offer evidence that an offence has been committed or might assist an escape from custody. The Drugs Act 2005 stipulates that police must obtain written consent from the individual to carry out an intimate search or take an X-ray or ultrasound scan to detect swallowed drugs. If consent is not given, a court can draw 'such inferences as appear proper'.

> **On-the-spot question**
>
> What are the implications for children and young people of the court being able to draw inferences from their refusal to consent to procedures within the police station?

Length of detention

PACE 1984 does not differentiate between adults and children with regards to the permitted length of detention before a charge is brought: all those arrested can be detained for an initial period of 24 hours, with an officer of at least the rank of superintendent being able to authorize a further 12 hours for **indictable offences**. The police must apply to the Magistrates' Court if they wish to extend the detention further than 36 hours to a maximum of 96 hours. Regular reviews of the need to keep the young person in police custody are required and should be noted in the custody record. This also allows an opportunity for the young person, solicitor or appropriate adult to raise any concerns about the young person's treatment.

A child or young person must be kept separate from adult suspects and must not be held in a cell unless no other secure accommodation is available and the custody officer considers it not practicable to supervise the child unless they are placed in a cell. However, many police stations only have one juvenile detention room, or none at all, and children are frequently put into adult cells (Hamilton, 2005). The Children Act 2004 requires police authorities and chief officers to cooperate with arrangements to improve the well-being of children with regards to their physical and mental health and protection from harm and neglect (Howard League for Penal Reform, 2013).

If the police need to obtain more evidence or advice before deciding how to deal with a case, they can release a suspect on bail, to return to the police station at a future date (s. 35(5) PACE 1984). The appropriate adult should retain a copy of the bail sheet to ensure the child knows the date and time of their bail date and the child must be accompanied by an appropriate adult on their return to the police station.

Decision to charge

After questioning and conducting any necessary searches (either on the street or in the police station), the police can decide whether to take no further action, bail the young person to return on another date, apply a YRD, issue the young person with a youth caution or YCC, or to charge the young person. Some areas operate a triage system, where the police and YOT consult over the decision to charge. If the young person is not charged, it is likely that they will be referred to the YOT or other specialist provision for an appropriate out-of-court intervention, which may include reparative activities or informal community resolutions (Pickford and Dugmore, 2012). The Legal Aid, Sentencing and Punishment of Offenders Act (LASPO) 2012 increased police discretion at this stage, allowing for more informal diversion from court, with the aim of ensuring that the outcome is proportionate to the offence, rather than automatically charging for the offence. LASPO 2012 also repealed the power to give a penalty notice for disorder to a person aged under 18 years.

Youth restorative disposals

The YRD was introduced to give police officers and PCSOs more discretion in responding to anti-social and nuisance offending, providing a quick, potentially restorative, response to low-level first offences as an alternative to arrest and formal criminal justice processing (DCSF, 2007). It was intended to provide a more efficient use of police time, improve public confidence in police interventions and to provide YOTs with an early opportunity to provide support and intervention to young people who may be at risk of becoming further involved in criminal or anti-social behaviour. A YRD can be applied to young people between the ages of 10 and 17 who have not previously received a youth caution or YCC (previously a reprimand or final warning). A young person may only receive one YRD; any further offending will be dealt with through established criminal justice measures. Serious crimes, such as sexual and drug offences or those involving weapons, are excluded. Both victim and alleged offender need to agree to participate in the YRD, which is facilitated by an authorized police officer or PCSO trained in restorative techniques. YRDs are recorded locally to ensure that young people are not issued with a further YRD, but to avoid disproportionate criminalization are not recorded on the Police National Computer. Children's Services and the YOT should be informed after the YRD is issued to provide an opportunity to identify early risk factors and co-ordinate appropriate support to the young person.

The YJB (2011) evaluation of the pilot YRDs found that three-quarters of YRDs were carried out 'instantly', 'on the street'. While officers favoured the attendance of parents/guardians, in practice this seldom happened. In most cases the YRD resulted in the outcome agreement being a verbal or written apology, although in a few cases financial compensation was also included. The lack of power to enforce outcome agreements was seen as a weakness by police, but potentially offers a safeguard against unfair outcomes for young people who do not have the protection of an appropriate adult or other legal safeguards. Restorative justice approaches are discussed further in Chapter 4.

Youth cautions and youth conditional cautions

LASPO 2012 replaced the previous system of reprimands and final warnings with a system of youth cautions and YCCs (previously introduced by the CJIA 2008). Youth cautions are available for all offences, although are primarily aimed at low-level offences, and can be offered on more than one occasion, to prevent young people from being propelled through the justice system. The CPS needs to authorize the use of youth cautions for indictable-only offences. YCCs can be used in the same way as youth cautions, but as a result of a joint decision between the police and the YOT, following an assessment of the young person. The YCC has mandatory conditions attached, which can include provisions that aim to rehabilitate, to provide reparation, or to punish. YOTs are responsible for monitoring the conditions and reporting wilful breaches to the police. A pilot scheme of YCCs found that, between January 2010 and March 2012, only 173 YCCs were issued in three of the five areas, which suggests they may not be popular with the police (Cavadino et al., 2013).

There is no statutory restriction on the number of youth cautions or YCCs that a young person can receive and they may receive a youth caution or YCC even if they have previous convictions. However, perhaps recognizing previous criticisms of repeat cautioning as ineffective (Audit Commission, 1996) and undermining confidence in the youth justice system (Marlow, 2005), the *Director's Guidance on Youth Conditional Cautions* (CPS, 2013) notes that a third YCC is unlikely to be effective in preventing offending and should not be offered as an alternative to prosecution.

The issuing of a youth caution or YCC to a young person requires their consent and their full recognition of guilt. There are concerns that some young people may accept a youth caution or YCC in a misguided attempt to avoid further action (particularly as they will be advised that failure to accept a YCC could result in prosecution), when they either have not been involved in the offence or where there may be insufficient evidence to secure a conviction (Ashworth and Redmayne, 2010). This may be heightened in the case of children and young people with emotional or behavioural difficulties, mental health disorders and/or learning disabilities. YCCs should only be given to young people aged 16 or under in the presence of an appropriate adult, which goes some way to countering such concerns, although the same protection needs to be extended to 17-year-olds.

On-the-spot question	What are the implications of increasing the powers of the police to deliver 'justice' on the streets, rather than in the courts?

Charge and prosecution

If the child is not entitled to receive a YRD, youth caution or YCC, and there is sufficient evidence for a prosecution, they will be charged with the offence by the custody officer, in the presence of the appropriate adult. Responsibility for the prosecution then passes to the CPS, which is required to determine whether there is sufficient evidence to continue with the case and whether prosecution is in the public interest. The CPS applies criteria set out in the Code for Crown Prosecutors, issued by the Director of Public Prosecutions under the Prosecution of Offenders Act 1985. The CPS can decide to discontinue prosecution proceedings at a later stage either because the available evidence is considered insufficiently strong or that it is not in the public interest to prosecute (Cavadino et al., 2013; see also further reading, below).

Police bail

After a child or young person is charged, their case will be committed to the court for trial and sentencing; in the interim period, police need to consider whether to grant bail. There should always be a presumption in favour of bail under the Bail Act 1976 and there are additional safeguards in relation to young people. The expectation is that the young person would be bailed unconditionally unless, as outlined in the CJPOA 1994:

- their correct name and address cannot be ascertained;
- there are reasonable grounds for the custody officer to consider that continued detention is necessary:
  - otherwise they will fail to appear at court;
  - for their own protection;
  - to prevent interference with the administration of justice or the investigation of offence(s);
  - to prevent them causing physical injury to any other person or from causing loss or damage to any property;
  - to prevent them committing an offence;
  - in the child's best interests (e.g. if the child is a drug addict or involved in prostitution).

In these cases, the police are required to transfer children to local authority accommodation unless it is impractical to do so (for example, because the roads are blocked by snow) (s. 38(6) PACE 1984). The YJB National

Standards (2013a) require local authorities to put in place arrangements for managing requests for accommodation from the police. The young person thereby becomes a looked after child and a referral should be made to the local authority to ensure that it is aware of the risk of detention. If no action is taken by the local authority and overnight detention seems likely, and it is considered that this could result in the child suffering serious harm, a child protection referral can be made (s. 47 Children Act 1989). If the prospect of overnight detention raises concerns about a child's general well-being, a child in need referral can be made to the local authority (s. 17 Children Act 1989).

Section 49 of the Criminal Justice Act 1991 amends s. 36(6) PACE 1984, enabling the police, in cases where a 15/16-year-old is charged with a violent or sexual offence, to refuse to enact a transfer to local authority accommodation unless it is to secure accommodation, if they believe that any other alternative would not be adequate to protect the public from serious harm. The local authority must satisfy itself that the criteria for a secure order are met and the young person can be held in secure accommodation for up to 72 hours.

Research has shown that children are often unnecessarily detained overnight in police cells: the Howard League for Penal Reform (2013) found that over 40,000 children aged under 17 were detained overnight in police cells in 2011, including 2292 children aged 10–13. The report found that police training on the overnight detention of children is limited and that there is a continued lack of awareness among some staff of the legal safeguards for children such that these measures are being ineffectively implemented. Evidence suggests that the law may be misinterpreted resulting in children being treated as adults and that custody officers lack awareness of the additional legal criteria for the use of secure accommodation under s. 25 Children Act 1989 (HM Inspectorate of Constabulary et al., 2011; Bell, 2013). Police should provide a certificate of juvenile detention for the court (s. 38(7) PACE 1984) indicating the actions taken and their reasons for doing so, but this is not always presented to the magistrates (Bell, 2013). Some local authorities also struggle to provide the accommodation required of them under s. 25 Children Act 1989 and/or fail to challenge the apparent need for secure accommodation for young people denied bail (HM Inspectorate of Constabulary et al., 2011). In practice, it has been found that the reciprocal duty 'on the police to transfer' and 'on the local authority to receive' children denied bail has been reduced to a brief telephone request for accommodation with a 'now standard response that "none is available"' (HM Inspectorate of Constabulary et al., 2011:9).

Conclusions

The initial contact children and young people have with the youth justice system is typically with the police: the outcome of such contact is highly influential on their potential progression through the system. The police have considerable discretion in their response to children and young people involved in offending behaviour, which can be beneficial for some, but it is imperative that this discretion is not discriminatory. The lack of data compiled on police contact with children and young people makes an accurate analysis of such interactions difficult and the extent of any discrimination in police responses to children and young people is unknown. The provision of an appropriate adult offers children and young people some support in safeguarding their rights and civil liberties while in the police station and the extension of this provision to 17-year-olds is to be lauded, although there is a lack of clarity over the role of the appropriate adults for 17-year-olds in, for example, consenting to searches or the taking of biometric data. It is also important that those appointed as appropriate adults do continue to safeguard and promote the welfare of the child, rather than just assuring compliance with PACE 1984 regulations.

Out-of-court disposals can be an important diversionary measure, but their use is not unproblematic and there are a lack of legal safeguards and few checks to guard against misuse or inappropriate use (Ellison, 2013). For example, children and young people may feel under pressure to accept a disposal or comply with the police requirements – perhaps without a full understanding of the consequences of doing so – and there may be no real opportunity to dispute the police interpretation of a specific situation. Diversionary interventions provide a semi-formal alternative to prosecution but risk net-widening: there is a concern that the police may use out-of-court disposals to deal with behaviour that is, objectively, not so serious that it needs to be subject to any criminal sanction, resulting in the unnecessary criminalization of children and young people. There may be occasions where the police are aware there is insufficient evidence for the CPS to charge and choose instead to offer the child or young person an out-of-court disposal (Law Society, 2012). There has been a considerable expansion of the police's legal powers to deliver 'justice' on the streets, potentially bypassing due process protections, and there is a need for the independent oversight of the use of out-of-court disposals. Such disposals are recorded by the police and may be cited in subsequent proceedings against a child or young person. Some diversionary activities may be less benign than they seem and impositions may not be proportionate to the harm caused or to sanctions that would have been given had the case progressed to trial.

The following chapter considers how the legal system responds to children and young people who are not involved in diversionary activities but who are charged by the CPS and face court hearings.

Further reading

CPS (undated) *Legal Guidance: Youth Offenders* details the principles underpinning the decision to prosecute, the roles of area youth justice coordinators and youth offender specialists, the handling of youth files, youth cautions and YCCs, and additional vulnerabilities that may need to be considered, such as learning disabilities or mental health concerns or looked after status.

MoJ (2011) *Achieving Best Evidence in Criminal Proceedings* provides guidance on interviewing victims and witnesses and on using special measures.

MoJ/YJB (undated/b) *Youth Out-of-Court Disposals: Guide for Police and Youth Offending Services* provides guidance on out-of-court disposals, including cautions and YRDs.

National Appropriate Adult Network is a registered charity and membership organization, but some areas of the website (including policy updates and publications) are free to access and contain guidance and information on the role of the appropriate adult www.appropriateadult.org.uk.

National Policing Improvement Agency (2012) *Guidance on the Safer Detention and Handling of Persons in Police Custody* focuses on practical issues such as the appropriate standards of care for individuals held in police custody, with a section devoted to children and young people.

YJB (2013a) *National Standards for Youth Justice Services* outline the standards expected for those working at all stages of the youth justice system.

3

IN THE YOUTH COURT

AT A GLANCE THIS CHAPTER COVERS:

- the court hierarchy
- trials and court processes
- remand decisions
- reviewing remand decisions and appeals against decisions
- discrimination and other tensions
- pre-sentence reports
- the right to anonymity

Following the outline of the processes by which children and young people come to court (arrest and police bail or summons) in Chapter 2, this chapter considers subsequent court hearings, the decision to remand a child or young person to local authority accommodation or on bail, and the role of the YOT in writing PSRs. Chapter 4 then outlines the sentences available to the court after a finding of guilt. The operation of the courts is governed by the Criminal Procedure Rules (issued and regularly updated by the MoJ (MoJ, undated)), which guide criminal case management, outline the explicit powers and responsibilities of courts in active case management and aim to reduce the numbers of ineffective hearings in courts.

The right to a fair trial

All court structures and processes should be underpinned by Article 6 ECHR and the Human Rights Act 1998:

Article 6

1. In the determination of his civil rights and obligations or of any criminal charge against him, everyone is entitled to a fair and public hearing within a reasonable time by an independent and impartial tribunal established by law. Judgment shall be pronounced publicly by the press and public may be excluded from all or part of the trial in the interest of morals, public order or national security in a democratic society, where the interests of juveniles or the protection of the private life of the parties so require, or the extent strictly necessary in the opinion of the court in special circumstances where publicity would prejudice the interests of justice.
2. Everyone charged with a criminal offence shall be presumed innocent until proved guilty according to law.
3. Everyone charged with a criminal offence has the following minimum rights:
    a) to be informed promptly, in a language which he understands and in detail, of the nature and cause of the accusation against him;
    b) to have adequate time and the facilities for the preparation of his defence;
    c) to defend himself in person or through legal assistance of his own choosing or, if he has not sufficient means to pay for legal assistance, to be given it free when the interests of justice so require;
    d) to examine or have examined witnesses against him and to obtain the attendance and examination of witnesses on his behalf under the same conditions as witnesses against him;

e) to have the free assistance of an interpreter if he cannot understand or speak the language used in court.

These rights are echoed in the UNCRC, in particular in Article 40(2)(b):

Article 40(2)

(b) Every child alleged as or accused of having infringed the penal law has at least the following guarantees:

  (i) To be presumed innocent until proven guilty according to law;

  (ii) To be informed promptly and directly of the charges against him or her, and, if appropriate, through his or her parents or legal guardians, and to have legal or other appropriate assistance in the preparation and presentation of his or her defence;

  (iii) To have the matter determined without delay by a competent, independent and impartial authority or judicial body in a fair hearing according to law, in the presence of legal or other appropriate assistance and, unless it is considered not to be in the best interest of the child, in particular, taking into account his or her age or situation, his or her parents or legal guardians.

Article 40(3) also provides for the 'establishment of laws, procedures, authorities and institutions specifically applicable to children alleged as, accused of, or recognized as having infringed the penal law', which supports the maintenance of a separate Youth Court for children and young people.

It is a principle of the youth justice system that cases will be concluded expeditiously and delays in the court process have led to appeals under the ECHR. For example, in *R (on the Application of AB) v Thames Youth Court* [2012], the non-attendance of key prosecution witnesses led to a delay of over 18 months between the commission of the offence and the hearing in the Youth Court. The appeal court upheld the young person's appeal against the decision to order a second adjournment, leading to the proceedings against him being dismissed.

The court hierarchy

The Youth Court

The juvenile court was first established by the Children Act 1908, with a dual function of hearing both civil and criminal proceedings for 10–16-year-old children. Under the Children Act 1989, civil responsibilities were transferred to the Family Proceedings Courts (now the Family Court); the remit of juvenile courts was extended to include 17-year-olds in the Criminal Justice Act 1991 and they were renamed Youth Courts. Thus, since 1989, the Youth Court has managed issues of bail, trial, sentencing and committal to the Crown Court for children aged 10–17. Decisions within the Youth Court are made either by three experienced lay magistrates, who form 'the bench', supported by a legal advisor, or less frequently, a legally qualified district judge, either alone or with two lay magistrates. The legal advisor is typically either a barrister or solicitor who advises the magistrates on points of law, but not on issues relating to the verdict or sentence, and who is also responsible for ensuring that cases are dealt with promptly and efficiently.

The Youth Court is less formal than an adult court, with a more informal physical layout. Only the child, parent/guardian or other appropriate adult, legal representative(s), members and officers of the court, witnesses, the press and other people authorized by the court are allowed in the courtroom (s. 47 CYPA 1933). The press is subject to tight restrictions, for example, not being allowed to identify any child involved in the proceedings (s. 49 CYPA 1933). The Youth Court emphasizes greater engagement with a young person and their parents (Allen et al., 2000; Home Office and Lord Chancellor's Department, 2001) and, following the riots in August 2011, the Youth Courts Committee published new guidance on reinforcing parental responsibility. A child under 16 must be accompanied to court by a parent/guardian unless there is good reason for them not attending. If the YOT is unable to persuade the parent(s) to attend, the court can require them to do so (s. 34a CYPA 1933), adjourning the hearing and issuing a summons if appropriate. The local authority has a duty to send a suitable representative if a child is looked after.

It is good practice for young people attending Youth Court hearings to be separated from adults attending adult hearings at all stages, with separate entrances, waiting rooms and courtrooms wherever possible. However, due to enhanced security measures and changing workload patterns within some court areas, there has been increased mixing of youth and adults in court buildings, leading to concerns that there is a serious risk of erosion of the protection given to young defendants appearing in Youth Courts (Bache, 2013). This can raise safeguarding issues for children and young people where potentially vulnerable defendants, victims and others are brought together in the Youth or Crown Court (HM Inspectorate of Probation et al., 2011).

The Crown Court

The Crown Court was established by the Courts Act 1971 to cope with the growing number of serious criminal cases, which had previously been heard by touring assize courts and by quarter sessions. Crown Courts are presided over by a judge, either a High Court judge, for the most serious cases, or a circuit judge or a recorder (part-time circuit judge), for less serious cases. Within the Crown Court a jury of 12 lay people decides whether the defendant is guilty on the basis of the facts presented; the judge decides on matters of law and sentencing. The Crown Court is an adult court but children and young people may be tried there if either there is an adult connection or if they are accused of a grave crime (discussed below). In 2009, 3410 children and young people aged 10–17 were tried in the Crown Court (MoJ, 2010).

The Crown Court is also the appeal court against refusal of bail, convictions and the sentence handed down by Magistrates' Courts, including Youth Courts. During an appeal, the Crown Court judge (usually sitting with two Youth Court magistrates, but no jury) re-hears the evidence that the witnesses have already given and may also hear new evidence. A conviction may be challenged on the grounds that it relied on a misinterpretation of the law or a wrongful finding of fact. A sentence may be contested on the grounds that it was excessive or too lenient; when sitting as an appeal court, the Crown Court may impose any sentence that the Youth Court could have ordered and may reduce or increase the severity of the sentence passed.

The High Court and appeals

The Queen's Bench Division of the High Court has a 'supervisory' juris-diction over Magistrates' Courts, including the Youth Court. A child may apply to the High Court for a judicial review of the lower court's decision if they consider that it has:

- acted irrationally or unreasonably;
- breached the rules of natural justice;
- gone beyond its statutory powers;
- wrongly exercised its discretion by taking into account irrelevant factors or ignoring factors that were relevant.

The defendant or, in some cases, the prosecution can, with permission, appeal against conviction and/or sentence in the Court of Appeal, which is staffed by the Lord Chief Justice, Lords of Appeal and High Court judges. After the appeals process has been exhausted, there is provision for a case to be referred to or taken up by the Criminal Cases Review Commission, which can decide to refer the case back to the Court of Appeal. If a defendant is unable to find a legal remedy to a perceived breach of their human rights under the Human Rights Act 1998, they may as a last resort apply to have their case heard by the European Court of Human Rights.

The prosecution has certain rights of appeal, which have expanded in recent years. The prosecution can appeal against the granting of bail in any court and, in more serious cases, the Attorney General can ask the Court of Appeal to review a sentence passed by the Crown Court that they consider to be unduly lenient (ss 57–67 CJA 2003), provided permission is given by the Crown Court judge or the Court of Appeal. The Director of Public Prosecutions may also apply to the Court of Appeal for an acquittal to be quashed and for a retrial to be ordered in cases involving specified serious offences such as murder and rape (ss 78–9 CJA 2003). There must be new and compelling evidence against the acquitted person and it must be in the interests of justice for the retrial to take place.

Determining jurisdiction

The core statutory provisions for determining the mode of trial for children and young people are set out in ss 24–5 Magistrates' Courts Act (MCA) 1980 and a 'welter of successive statutory amendments' such that 'there is no fully comprehensive, authoritative statement to date of the procedure to be followed' (Stone, 2010a:81), leading to a number of appeals (see key case analysis). Under the MCA 1980, a young person aged under 18 will be tried summarily unless they are charged with homicide, designated firearms offences or grave crimes included in the Powers of the Criminal Courts (Sentencing) Act (PCC(S)A) 2000, where the court considers that there is a realistic prospect that a sentence greater than that available in the Youth Court would be imposed, in which case they will be tried in the Crown Court. Children and young people who are charged jointly with an adult (aged 18 or over) will be tried in an adult court and may be committed to the Crown Court (discussed later). In determining mode of trial, magistrates can consider both the seriousness of the alleged offence in the light of alleged associated offences and the defendant's previous convictions (*R (on the Application of Tullet) v Medway Magistrates' Court* [2003]). If a case is sent to the Crown Court and the anticipated plea is not guilty, the case will be listed for a Plea and Case Management Hearing; if a guilty plea is anticipated, an earlier date and a request for a PSR would be appropriate.

Once a decision regarding jurisdiction has been made, it cannot be reconsidered, even if new material emerges, unless it appears to the court before the conclusion of the prosecution's evidence that the case ought not be tried summarily (s. 25 MCA 1980). This applies only where the Magistrates' Court has embarked upon a summary trial in the narrow sense of determining guilt or innocence (*R v Dudley Justices, ex parte Gillard* [1986], applied in *R v Herefordshire Youth Court, ex parte J* [1998]). There is no scope to reconsider venue following a guilty plea, regardless of whether further information is presented concerning the defendant's circumstances, attitudes or antecedents, as upheld in *R (on the Application of D) v Sheffield Youth Court* [2008] (see Stone, 2010a).

> **KEY CASE ANALYSIS**

R (on the Application of T) v Bromley Youth Court [2014]: determining jurisdiction

The claimant (T) was a 14-year-old girl who was jointly charged, with three other young people, with a robbery during which the 16-year-old victim sustained moderate injuries. The claimant was at the time of good character. Notwithstanding submissions from T's solicitor that the matter should be tried in the Youth Court, the lay magistrates decided to allocate the matter to the Crown Court because the matter was so serious that the provisions of s. 24 MCA 1980 and s. 91 PCC(S)A 2000 applied because the magistrates considered that long-term detention was a realistic possibility. At a Plea and Case Management Hearing in the Crown Court, T pleaded not guilty but her co-defendants all pleaded guilty so T would have had to stand trial alone.

At the start of the trial HHJ Ainley expressed concern that T, who was still only 14 years old, was facing trial as a single defendant in the Crown Court. Defence counsel asked that no jury should be sworn that afternoon so that further investigations could take place as to why she had been sent to the Crown Court for trial.

The appeal held that, in the light of the age, previous good record and role of T, a sentence exceeding two years would have been manifestly excessive and failed to take account of all the relevant sentencing principles. As such, the decision to commit the case to the Crown Court was quashed and the case remitted back to the Youth Court.

Thus, if a child is charged with murder or homicide, the case will be remitted to the Crown Court for trial. If the charge relates to one of the other offences which can trigger the grave crimes provisions ('**triable-either way**'), the young person will first appear in the Youth Court where magistrates determine whether to accept or decline jurisdiction. Where jurisdiction is retained, the case remains in the Youth Court and is subject to the usual procedures and sentences (see also Chapter 4).

The statutory framework delineates a large category of offences that may, at the discretion of the court, be considered a grave crime in a particular instance. What constitutes a grave crime is significantly broader than the common use of the term and the category of offences for which the grave crime provisions can be invoked has widened significantly as a result of changes to the sentencing structure for adults (NACRO, 2002) and the extension of s. 91 PCC(S)A 2000 sentences to children aged 10–13. The core principle remains, however, that wherever possible young people, and particularly those aged under 15, should be dealt with by the Youth Court (Stone, 2010a).

Where cases involve serious sexual assaults, the Protocol on Rape Cases in the Youth Court 2007 details the scope for a circuit judge to be assigned to conduct the trial within the Youth Court (under the Courts Act 2003), so that a professional judge with specialist experience can try the case whilst retaining the advantages of a Youth Court (Stone, 2010a). However, other factors (for example, the potential for a longer sentence being appropriate and the right of the defendant to trial by jury) must also be considered and magistrates must not simply defer to the Protocol (Stone, 2010a).

As noted above, cases against children and young people who are charged with a **summary offence** jointly with an adult (aged 18 or over) will be heard in an adult court (s. 46 CYPA 1933; see also *R v Tottenham Youth Court, ex parte Fawzy* [1999]). Where both the adult and young person plead not guilty, the trial will proceed before the adult court. Where an adult pleads guilty but a child does not, the magistrates have discretion whether to retain jurisdiction for the trial or to remit to the Youth Court (s. 29 MCA 1980). The adult court's powers of sentence are restricted to a referral order, discharge or fine; if any other sentence is considered appropriate, the case must be remitted to the Youth Court (s. 8 PCC(S)A 2000).

Where a young person and adult are charged with an indictable offence, the court has a discretionary power to send the young person's

> **KEY CASE ANALYSIS**

CPS v South East Surrey Youth Court (Ghanbari as Interested Party) [2006]: determining jurisdiction and the trial of children charged with adults

The CPS brought an application for judicial review of a decision by the defendant justices to proceed with the summary trial of the interested party (M) on a charge of assault occasioning actual bodily harm. The CPS invited the Youth Court to send M to the Crown Court for trial under s. 51A(3)(d) CDA 1998 on the grounds that the alleged offence was a specified violent offence within the meaning of s. 224(3) CJA 2003 and that there was a real possibility that the criteria for the imposition of an extended sentence under s. 228(2) would be met. The justices considered guidance from their clerk, identifying a conflict between s. 51A(3)(d) CDA 1998 and s. 24 MCA 1980. They concluded that assault occasioning actual bodily harm was not a grave crime, so as to satisfy s. 24(1) MCA 1980, that they ought not to consider the provisions of s. 51A(3)(d) CDA 1998, and that the case remained within their summary jurisdiction. M entered a plea of not guilty and the case was adjourned for a pre-trial review.

The application was refused on the grounds that although there was a conflict between the provisions of s. 24(1) MCA 1980 and those of s. 51A CDA 1998, it was not open to a Youth Court to ignore either provision. When considering the applicability of the two inconsistent provisions to a particular case, justices should bear in mind the policy of the legislature that those under 18 should, wherever possible, be tried in a Youth Court that was best designed for their specific needs; *R (on the Application of H) v Southampton Youth Court* [2004] applied.

Additionally, the court held that when a youth under 18 is jointly charged with an adult, an exercise of judgment will be called for by the Youth Court when assessing the competing presumptions in favour of (a) joint trial of those jointly charged and (b) the trial of youths in the Youth Court. Factors relevant to that judgment will include: the age and maturity of the youth; the comparative culpability in relation to the offence and the previous convictions of the two; and whether the trial can be severed without either injustice or undue inconvenience to witnesses.

The latter finding was further supported in a consultation paper published by the Sentencing Council (2011).

case to the Crown Court (s. 24(1)(b) MCA 1980). The young person does not have a right to trial at the Crown Court but the Magistrates' Court will hear representations from the prosecution and defence on 'interests of justice' considerations (Stone, 2012). If the court determines that it is not necessary to try the young person and adult jointly (see key case analysis), the court will take the young person's plea. If it is a guilty plea, the sentencing limitations outlined above will apply; if the young person enters a not guilty plea, the MCA 1980 provides that before any evidence is called the court may remit the case for trial in the Youth Court (Stone, 2012).

When a young person is convicted at the Crown Court, the court can remit them to the Youth Court for sentencing or retain jurisdiction. Long-term detention is available under the PCC(S)A 2000, up to the same maximum penalty as would be available in the case of an adult, in addition to all orders that the Youth Court might impose.

On-the-spot questions

1 In what circumstances might it be appropriate for a child or young person to be tried in an adult court?
2 What are the implications of doing so?

Trials and court processes

A child or young person charged and refused bail by the police will be required to attend the first appropriate Youth Court hearing, otherwise they will be summonsed to appear in the Youth Court on a set date. Depending on whether the child accepts or denies guilt, the case will be adjourned for sentence or trial. Committal hearings were abolished nationally in May 2013 as part of wider measures to improve efficiencies in the justice system, so cases are now sent straight to the Crown Court as soon as it is clear the matter is serious enough for the Youth Court to decline jurisdiction, rather than having to await a committal hearing.

Children and young people appearing in court after charge should be able to access free legal advice, with a defence solicitor being appointed to advise the young person as to the court process, the evidence against them, issues of bail and their plea. The defence solicitor should liaise with the YOT regarding the possibility of bail being denied (particularly if a secure remand is likely) and regarding the PSR (discussed below).

Magistrates and district judges presiding over hearings in the Youth Court receive specialist training to facilitate their understanding of youth justice legislation and the additional factors that need to be considered when conducting Youth Court trials. However, there are no such requirements for Crown Court judges, who often have little experience of hearing cases involving children and young people (Independent Parliamentarians' Inquiry, 2014). Furthermore, unlike the system within family law where only solicitors on an approved list can act for children, there is no requirement for lawyers representing children in criminal cases to have any specialist knowledge or skills (Hart, 2014). The Youth Court is often used as a place for legal practitioners to 'cut their teeth', despite youth justice cases frequently being more complex and specialized than adult cases (Independent Parliamentarians' Inquiry, 2014). This can lead to children and young people being poorly advised or represented, with adverse consequences for both remand and sentencing decisions.

Effective participation

The judiciary have a responsibility to strike a balance under Article 6 ECHR between protecting the defendant's right to a fair trial and ensuring that all witnesses, including those who are vulnerable or intimidated, are enabled to give their best evidence. There is a general recognition in law that defendants must be able to understand and participate effectively in criminal proceedings (Article 6 ECHR and associated case law). The requirement for effective participation is also reflected in the criteria used to determine 'fitness to plead', namely that the defendant can plead with understanding, can follow the proceedings, know a juror can be challenged, can question the evidence and can instruct counsel. Under the Equality Act 2010, courts must ensure that discrimination against people with disabilities does not occur by providing the necessary practical assistance and facilities, or 'reasonable adjustments', to facilitate their effective participation. The Disability Discrimination Act 1995 defines a disabled person as someone who has 'a physical or mental impairment which has a substantial and long-term adverse effect on his ability to carry out normal day-to-day activities'. This definition can encompass mental health problems and learning, developmental or behavioural disorders such as autism, ADHD, communication difficulties, and dyslexia, all of which are conditions likely to make additional support in court necessary.

Ensuring the effective participation of child defendants can be especially complex (Independent Parliamentarians' Inquiry, 2014). Approximately a quarter of children who offend have an IQ of less than 70 and over 60 per cent have communication difficulties, half of whom have poor or very poor communication skills. These children may have limited language ability and comprehension skills, finding it difficult to understand and respond to questions; they may take longer to process information or have difficulty recalling information; they may be more suggestible and, under pressure, may try to appease other people (Prison Reform Trust, 2012). A failure to make appropriate adjustments in court to account for these enhanced vulnerabilities may result in the denial of the right to a fair trial.

The European Court of Human Rights ruled, in December 1999, that, as children, Robert Thompson and Jon Venables were denied a fair trial in the Crown Court, in breach of Article 6.1 ECHR, as they were unable to participate effectively in the proceedings (see also Article 40 UNCRC). A range of special measures for young defendants appearing in the Crown Court have since been implemented, following a Practice Direction on the Trial of Children and Young Persons in the Crown Court 2000 and subsequent guidance. Courts are required to have regard to the welfare of the child and to avoid exposing the child, so far as possible, to intimidation, humiliation or distress. All possible steps should be taken to assist a young defendant to understand and participate in the proceedings, including using appropriate language during proceedings and allowing children to sit with their families in a location that facilitates communication with their legal representatives. Court staff should not wear robes and wigs, there should be no recognizable police presence in the courtroom and, while the court remains public, the numbers attending should be limited.

Whilst the Practice Direction aimed to improve the court experience for young defendants, it did not entitle them to the same consideration given to children and young people appearing as witnesses in court hearings, nor did it consider the particular needs of children with learning difficulties or other impairments. While the YJCE 1999 provided special measures for vulnerable witnesses (including screening from the accused, giving evidence by live-link or in private, pre-recorded evidence-in-chief, the use of an intermediary and other aids to communication), these provisions were not made available to young defendants. Arguably, this breached the fundamental principle of 'equality of arms' under Article 6 ECHR (Stone, 2010b; Prison Reform Trust, 2012).

Following a number of legal cases and a governmental review of child evidence (Bradley Report, 2009; Stone, 2010b), s. 47 Police and Justice Act 2006 amended the YJCE 1999 to allow a limited group of vulnerable defendants to give evidence via live-link, where the court is satisfied that it is in the interests of justice and that the young person's ability to participate effectively as a witness giving oral evidence is compromised by their level of intellectual ability or social functioning and the use of a live-link would enable more effective participation. Section 104 Coroners and Justice Act 2009 further amends the YJCE 1999, enabling the court to direct that certain vulnerable defendants may be assisted by an intermediary when they give evidence in court, if this is necessary to ensure that the accused receives a fair trial (see key case analysis).

Further recognition of the needs of young defendants was made in an amendment to the Consolidated Criminal Practice Direction 2008, regarding the treatment of 'vulnerable defendants', including those aged under 18, in both Crown Court and Magistrates' Court proceedings. The direction stated that consideration should be given to: a separate trial, if jointly charged with a non-vulnerable co-defendant; providing an out-of-hours familiarization visit to the court; and allowing the defendant to sit with their family and/or a supporting adult (such as a social worker) during the trial, and near to their legal representatives. The court should take account of the defendant's ability to concentrate and have appropriate breaks and ensure that simple, clear language is used during the trial, including during cross-examination (Stone, 2010b). The Practice Direction on special measures for young defendants in court proceedings became a mandatory part of the Criminal Procedure Rules in October 2013 and the Coalition government has made a commitment to developing liaison and diversion services across England, including working with criminal justice staff to identify vulnerable defendants and address their particular support needs (Prison Reform Trust, 2012).

Nonetheless, there remains a lack of equality of arms in relation to the measures that are available for young victims and witnesses and those available for young defendants. In particular, a judicial review has been lodged to challenge the inadequacy of arrangements for defendants' court intermediaries (CRAE, 2013). Caution also needs to be taken when considering the benefits of employing the special measures – for example, in a personal reflection, the Chair of the Youth Courts Committee of the Magistrates' Association John Bache (2013) argued that, although video-enabled courts have logistical and financial advantages and enable

> **KEY CASE ANALYSIS**

C v Sevenoaks Youth Court [2009]: special measures for vulnerable defendants

C, aged 11, was charged with assaulting another young person with intent to rob him of his mobile phone. C displayed serious mental health problems and was assessed, on the instruction of his solicitor, by a clinical psychologist who reported that he was severely over-active, had extremely poor concentration and low tolerance, and a level of comprehension considerably below his chronological age. He had a diagnosis of ADHD, symptoms of Asperger syndrome and was unable to understand others' emotional state or non-verbal communication (Stone, 2010b). A further assessment by a consultant forensic neuro-psychiatrist confirmed a diagnosis of autistic spectrum disorder and hyperkinetic neuro-developmental syndrome, with an impaired capacity to assimilate information or to form coherent conclusions. C had particular difficulty with abstract thinking and presenting events or ideas in a logical order. The clinical psychologist considered that C would be able to manage the basic demands of being tried, if simple language was used and regular breaks provided, but that he would not be able to concentrate effectively, listen to the evidence, instruct his solicitor, or cope with cross-examination. The clinical psychologist advised that C should have a court-appointed intermediary to enable his effective participation such that the trial could proceed. The court made such an order but, following advice from the justices' clerk that it might not have the power to do so, ultimately revoked the order on the basis that the YJCE 1999 did not apply to defendants.

C sought judicial review; the Divisional Court determined that the appointment of an intermediary in C's case was entirely appropriate, in line with the Criminal Procedure Rules 2005 (MoJ, undated), Article 6 ECHR, and previous case decisions (see Stone, 2010b). In addition, Openshaw J stated that, in order for an intermediary to be effective, a young defendant must have the opportunity to meet them in advance to establish some basis of trust.

It is arguable, however, whether it was appropriate to consider that any child with such a high level of disturbance and disorder should be dealt with by the youth justice system, or whether diversionary, multi-agency intervention is more appropriate (Stone, 2010b).

defendants to give evidence via live-link, they may severely compromise the direct engagement of magistrates with the young person, which is seen as fundamental to the underlying principles of youth justice (see also the Law Society, 2012). The Nuffield Foundation (2011) has funded an empirical research study of the impact of special measures on jury decision-making, due to be completed in 2015, in response to concerns among the judiciary that special measures may be having a counter-productive effect on juries in some circumstances.

On-the-spot questions	1 What are the advantages and disadvantages of special measures for young defendants?
	2 Should young defendants and young victims be offered access to the same special measures?

Remand decisions

When a child or young person appears in court for the first time, the court must either hear the case or adjourn it until it can be heard. Similarly an adjournment may be necessary between conviction and sentencing, to allow a PSR to be prepared, or pending an appeal. During the adjournment, the young person will usually be bailed, either with or without conditions (Johns, 2011). Part of the role of the YOT is to reduce the likelihood of bail being refused through the provision of services that can address the objections to bail. In the event that bail is withheld, the YOT's assessment contributes to the decision about where the child will be placed. The CDA 1998 details the services that are to be provided/coordinated by YOTs, including support for children and young people on remand, overseeing remand placements in local authority accommodation, and providing reports and assessments to the court to aid the remand decision-making process. Whilst court hearings involving children and young people are meant to be conducted in an expeditious manner, the remand period may last from a week to 6 months or more, with the average length of time spent on remand in custody being 45 days (MoJ, 2014). Some young people may spend much longer on remand, particularly if they are being tried alongside an adult. The decision made by the magistrates will therefore have signifi-cant consequences for the young person, not only in terms of future decisions made within the justice process, but also in terms of the influ-ences exerted upon the young person whilst they are on remand.

There is a long-standing presumption that any person charged with an offence is presumed innocent until proven otherwise and, as such, should not be punished or deprived of any rights that pertain to a non-accused person (King and Morgan, 1976; Article 6 ECHR). Historically, there has been a legal presumption in favour of bail with the burden of proof lying with the prosecution, such that the prosecution should have to justify a remand to custody rather than the accused having to defend their right to bail. However, there was a slow erosion of the rights of defendants over the latter part of the twentieth century, with the presumption of bail being curtailed in certain situations (Lipscombe, 2006) and more control being exerted over those on remand. For example, the Criminal Justice and Police Act 2001 allowed the use of electronic tagging for young people aged 12 or over remanded on bail, including those remanded to local authority accommodation.

The Bail Act 1976 states that the general exceptions to the right of bail are that the court has substantial grounds for believing the accused would:

1 fail to answer bail;
2 commit further offences on bail;
3 interfere with witnesses or otherwise obstruct the course of justice.

Defendants may also be remanded in custody for their own protection, or, in the case of a child or young person, for their own welfare.

As with all decision-making, the court must have regard to the welfare of the youth (s. 44 CYPA 1933; see also Article 37 UNCRC regarding deprivation of liberty, and Chapter 5). There is also a corresponding duty to have regard to the principal aim of the youth justice system – to prevent offending (s. 37 CDA 1998) – when considering representations in respect of bail.

Bail may be granted either with or without conditions. Conditions may be imposed by the court to ensure that children awaiting trial or sentencing complete their time on bail 'successfully' – by returning to court when required and by not committing offences whilst on bail. The court may also impose a condition on a child or young person 'for his own welfare or in his own interests' (s. 3(6) Bail Act 1976). Bail supervision and support schemes, run by the YOT, local authority social workers or voluntary agencies, exist in most areas for children and young people. Bail support is, at its simplest, 'the provision of services designed to facilitate the granting of bail where bail would otherwise be denied'

(NACRO, 1998:2). The schemes typically include a programme of community-based activities, provided by the scheme or through referral to specialist organizations, and aim to improve social and life skills, develop anger-management strategies, reduce drug and alcohol misuse and tackle difficulties with family relationships, education, employment or accommodation. Children and young people aged 12–17 may also be granted bail with ISS (see also Chapter 4), or electronic monitoring ('tagging') if they have been charged with or convicted of a violent or sexual offence, an offence punishable in the case of an adult with imprisonment for a term of 14 years or more; or if they are charged with or have been convicted of one or more imprisonable offences and have a recent history of repeatedly committing imprisonable offences while remanded on bail or to local authority accommodation; and electronic monitoring is deemed suitable for that child or young person (s. 3AA Bail Act 1976).

Remand to local authority accommodation

LASPO 2012 has simplified existing legislation regarding remands to local authority accommodation, court-ordered secure remands and remands to custody, removing the previous differentiation between boys aged 15 and 16 and girls aged 12 to 17, such that all children aged 12–17 are treated the same for remand purposes, regardless of their gender.

If bail is refused, a child or young person must be remanded to local authority accommodation (s. 91(3) LASPO 2012) or remanded to youth detention accommodation (s. 91(4) LASPO 2012; see below). The court designates the local authority that is to receive the child: if the child is already looked after, that authority; or the local authority where it appears that the child habitually resides or the offence was committed. All children remanded to local authority accommodation are given the status of 'looked after' and are entitled to the same resources and provisions as other looked after children.

A court remanding a child to local authority accommodation may require the child to comply with any conditions that could be imposed under s. 3(6) Bail Act 1976 if the child were being granted bail. The court may also impose requirements on the designated authority for securing compliance with any conditions imposed on the child and/or a requirement stipulating that the child must not be placed with a named person. The placement is at the discretion of the authority: the young person could be placed in a residential unit, with foster carers or returned home.

Finding appropriate accommodation can be problematic due to limited resources within some areas (see, for example, Thomas, 2005; Lipscombe, 2006).

Children aged 10 to 11 who are refused bail

Young people aged 10 and 11 cannot be remanded to secure accommodation, so a refusal to grant bail results in a remand to local authority accommodation. Where a court remands a 10 or 11-year-old who is either charged with or has been convicted of a serious offence or, in the opinion of the court, is a persistent offender, the court may order the local authority to make an oral or written report specifying where the child is likely to be placed or maintained if he or she is remanded into local authority accommodation (s. 23b Children and Young Persons Act 1969). The court can impose conditions on the remand, but cannot impose a security requirement. However, the local authority can subsequently apply to the court for a secure accommodation order under s. 25 Children Act 1989, once bail has been refused, for any young person aged 10 to 16. The court may grant such an order if it finds:

s. 25(1)

    (a) that
        (i)   he has a history of absconding and is likely to abscond from any other description of accommodation; and
        (ii) if he absconds, he is likely to suffer significant harm; or
    (b) if he is kept in any other description of accommodation he is likely to injure himself or other persons.

Children Act 1989

Remand to youth detention accommodation

Children and young people aged 12 to 17 who are refused bail may be remanded to youth detention accommodation, a generic term than encompasses court-ordered secure remands and remands in custody. The YJB placement service, rather than the court, now determines whether to place a young person aged 12 to 17 on remand in a secure children's home, STC or young offender institution (YOI), depending on assessments of risk, needs, individual circumstances and the availability of beds.

    A remand to youth detention can be ordered if one of two conditions are met, either:

- the offence is either a violent or sexual offence, or one that, if committed by an adult, is punishable with a sentence of imprisonment of 14 years or more; or
- there is a 'realistic prospect' of receiving a custodial sentence *and* the young person has a recent history of committing offences or absconding while on remand.

The court must, after considering all of the available options, be of the opinion that only remanding the child to youth detention accommodation would be adequate to protect the public from death or serious personal injury (whether physical or psychological) occasioned by further offences committed by the child, or to prevent the commission by the child of imprisonable offences. The child must be legally represented, unless representation was provided to the child under LASPO 2012, but was withdrawn because of the child's conduct, the child was not eligible for such representation, or having been informed of the right to apply for such representation and having had the opportunity to do so, the child refused or failed to apply.

In line with moves towards cost-efficiency, payment-by-results and incentivizing the decreased use of custody, the costs of youth detention accommodation will be transferred to local authorities; many local authorities will not welcome the additional costs of remands to youth

---

PRACTICE FOCUS

David, aged 15, has been charged with robbery after he threatened another boy with a knife and stole his mobile phone. David has been diagnosed with ADHD and has moderate hearing loss. The prosecution has argued that the robbery should be considered as a grave crime and that the trial should be conducted in the Crown Court. David denies his involvement in the offence so a full trial will be necessary.

- What are the implications for David if the case is heard in the Crown Court?
- On what grounds could a Youth Court hearing be justified as an alternative to the Crown Court?
- What measures should be taken to ensure David can effectively participate in the trial?
- What remand options are available to the court, pending the start of the trial?

detention and this may exacerbate tensions between the welfare and justice systems (Fox and Arnull, 2013). The court must designate the local authority responsible for accommodating the child and, as with remands to local authority accommodation, the child or young person will be given looked after status.

Care planning

The court-designated local authority has to fulfil certain statutory requirements for young people who are remanded, including visiting and establishing a care plan for the duration of their remand (YJB, 2013c). Where these children are remanded to local authority accommodation there is little change to established care-planning processes. Where a child is remanded to youth detention accommodation, the amended regulations require that the authority responsible for their care prepares a detention placement plan (Care Planning, Placement and Case Review (England) (Miscellaneous Amendments) Regulations 2013).

A young person who is 'technically remanded' (serving a custodial sentence, but also facing charges for other offences) should be treated as a looked after child, although the designated authorities will not be charged for the cost of technical remand periods. Once the young person is convicted, the responsibility for them is transferred to the YJB and, although a social worker may still be involved, the duty of care is transferred to the secure environment. This highlights some of the philosophical, practical and financial divisions between youth justice and welfare (Fox and Arnull, 2013) and requires a collaborative and partnership-working approach to be implemented to ensure the young person is fully supported.

Reviewing remand decisions and appeals against decisions

Given the presumption in favour of bail, the court is, in theory, required to consider the child's remand status at each hearing. In practice, however, if the prosecution objects to bail, the defence is required to make a bail application. Whilst for adults, the defence can make two applications as of right, after which the court is not obliged to reconsider arguments that have previously been heard unless there is a change of circumstances, the need to consider the child's welfare includes a specific obligation to reconsider a bail application at further hearings (*R (on the Application of B) v Brent Youth Court* [2010].

Where children are refused bail, they can appeal to the Crown Court, with the case being heard by a judge in chambers as opposed to a full court hearing. It is also open to the prosecution to appeal if bail is granted in a case involving an imprisonable offence (Bail (Amendment) Act 1993). In this event, the CPS gives verbal notice to the Youth Court at the end of proceedings. The effect of such a notice is that the child is automatically refused bail until the appeal is heard by the Crown Court.

Discrimination and other tensions

Research has consistently demonstrated that the discrimination and inequalities evident elsewhere in the criminal justice system are replicated in the remand decision and that disadvantage and social injustice can undermine a defendant's right to a fair hearing (Reiner, 1985; Fitzgerald, 1993; Ashworth and Redmayne, 2010). There is a significant over-representation of black and minority ethnic children on remand in custodial institutions (Children's Society, 2000a; 2000b) and girls may be similarly over-represented (Ashworth and Redmayne, 2010). Furthermore, being remanded to custody can increase the likelihood of being found guilty and receiving a custodial sentence, although there is disagreement as to why (Winfield, 1984), possibly being related to the preparation of a legal defence, the appearance in court via video-link or under escort by prison officials, or presumptions made by the judiciary – the assumption of guilt because a remand to youth detention was deemed necessary or because the primary decision was based on the grounds that there was a 'realistic prospect' of receiving a custodial sentence.

There are also concerns when a child or young person's first bail application is heard within an adult Magistrates' Court, for example, if the child is co-accused with an adult, or if a Youth Court is not sitting and the first available hearing post-arrest is within an adult 'Saturday' court (Independent Parliamentarians' Inquiry, 2014); the latter may become more problematic in light of the Coalition government's White Paper, *Swift and Sure Justice* (MoJ, 2012), which encourages the use of weekend courts. Magistrates in Youth Courts receive specialist training about the provision for juveniles whilst magistrates in adult courts may not be aware of the alternatives for young people in the area; YOT staff may not always be present in adult court hearings or may not take the initiative in presenting alternative bail support packages to the court (HM

Inspectorate of Probation et al., 2011) and, as discussed above, the quality of legal representation for children and young people appearing in court may be questionable.

Pre-sentence reports

Children and young people may be remanded on bail, to local authority accommodation or youth detention between conviction and sentencing to allow the preparation of a PSR, defined in CJA 2003 as a report which:

s. 158(1)

    (a) with a view to assisting the court in determining the most suitable method of dealing with an offender, is made or submitted by an appropriate officer, and

    (b) contains information as to such matters, presented in such manner, as may be prescribed by rules made by the Secretary of State.

CJA 2003

Children or young people facing custody must have a PSR before a discretionary custodial sentence can be imposed (s. 156 CJA 2003). Preparation for the PSR may include an assessment of risk or need, including assessments of vulnerability, mental health or an assessment of the risk of serious harm (which may inform a MAPPA risk management plan; see Chapter 4). The PSR assessment may be informed by ONSET or ASSET/ASSETPlus assessments (Chapter 1). The YJB stipulates that all PSRs should include an assessment of the need for parenting support and, if relevant, consider whether the court should impose a parenting order (s. 8 CDA 1998; see also Chapter 1). Reflecting the increased emphasis on restorative justice (Chapter 4), PSRs should also consider whether restorative interventions may be appropriate. The YJB *National Standards* (2013c) also state that reports must be balanced, impartial, timely, focused, free from discriminatory language and stereotypes, verified, factually accurate and intelligible to the child or young person and their parents/carers. In addition, they should provide the required level of information and analysis to enable sentencers to make informed decisions about sentencing options. The PSR should be shown to the young person or their legal representative and the court must also give a copy to their parent or guardian (s. 159(2)(a) and (b) CJA 2003).

However, *Not Making Enough Difference,* a critical joint report by HM Inspectorate of Probation and others (2011), found that many young people and their parents only saw the PSR on the hearing date, accompanied by a quick run-through by their solicitor. PSRs were also found to have a very limited analysis of the offence and insufficient detail on the young person's response to previous sentences, where applicable. The report further criticized the lack of significance given to the young person's maturity in many PSRs: 'the lack of consideration of age, child development and adolescence was so distinct in some reports that they could have been written about adults' (HM Inspectorate of Probation et al., 2011:49). The report reiterated the importance of good quality PSRs, providing the court with robust evidence to support the imposition of the most appropriate order, drawing on knowledge of the law, child development and current research, and on the sentences that are available to the court (see Chapters 4 and 5).

As alternatives to a full PSR, there are two types of expedited reports: a stand-down report, prepared on the day in court, and a sentence specific report (SSR), requested by the sentencing court in consideration of a specific sentence. SSRs can be completed on the day of the hearing, or exceptionally within 5 working days. The perceived need to complete a full ASSET in line with the scaled approach and youth rehabilitation orders (YROs) has led to a reduction in the number of stand-down reports (HM Inspectorate of Probation et al., 2011).

The right to anonymity

Other than those subject to an ASBO/IPNA, children and young people appearing in the Youth Court have the automatic right to have their anonymity preserved, although this can be waived under s. 49 CYPA 1933: to avoid injustice to the child; to assist with finding a child defendant who is 'at large' if they have been charged with a serious violent or sexual offence; or, where a child has been convicted, it is deemed to be in the public interest – usually following an application by the media. There is no right to anonymity in Crown Courts, although it can be requested by the defence and granted under s. 39 CYPA 1933 if the judge decides it to be appropriate. Evidence suggests that allowing children to be identified can lead to a risk of physical attack, sexual exploitation and psychological or emotional harm, stigmatization and bullying, not only to the identified child but also to their siblings and other family members (Hart, 2014).

There are legal routes for protecting children's identities other than the CYPA 1933, such as the Contempt of Court Act 1981, which can be used to restrict reporting that could prejudice criminal proceedings, and the High Court can issue injunctions or reporting restriction orders, although it is rare for them to be used in cases involving child defendants (Hart, 2014). It is crucial that the YOT working with the child is notified when consideration is being given to naming a child, but evidence suggests that this does not routinely occur – the YOT may only be made aware of the application on the day of sentencing (if at all), making it impossible to make a representation to the court (Hart, 2014).

Failing to protect the anonymity of children breaches their rights under the Human Rights Act 1998 and the UNCRC. For example, anonymity only applies to children once they have been charged with an offence, so they may be publicly identified at an earlier point, while the case is being investigated, which may detrimentally affect their right to a fair hearing. Public identification also breaches a child's right to privacy and is unlikely to be in their best interests. The UN Committee on the Rights of the Child (2008) criticized the UK for not taking sufficient measures to protect children from negative media representation and recommended that the UK should cooperate with the media to respect the privacy of children and not publicly expose them through 'naming and shaming'. However, the government appears to have made no moves towards implementing this recommendation. For example, following the 2011 riots, the Home Secretary, Theresa May, said that she wanted the CPS, where possible, to ask for the anonymity of children found guilty of criminal activity to be lifted (Hart, 2014).

A further challenge arises because the CYPA 1933 only applies to children aged under 18. If a defendant reaches the age of 18 during their hearing, neither s. 49 nor s. 39 can be used to give them anonymity. Furthermore, ruling in a High Court case, pursued by several major media organizations (*JC and Another v Central Criminal Court* [2014]), Lord Justice Leveson ruled that the anonymity provided to children under s. 39 CYPA 1933 automatically expires at age 18, which means that they can be retrospectively identified, even where these cases have long since concluded and the child has served their sentence. However, in his written judgment, Leveson called on Parliament to 'fashion a solution … as a matter of urgency', recognizing the inherent dangers to those involved in the justice system as children, both as offenders and as victims; leave to appeal the judgment is being sought.

Conclusions

Although court processes are governed by clear legal standards, it is apparent that these standards are not always implemented equitably, with concerns about the quality of legal representation for children and young people, both in the police station and in court. There is a need to address the equality of arms for defendants and victims to ensure that all parties can participate effectively in court hearings, including those with communication difficulties, mental health problems, learning, developmental or behavioural disorders, and physical disabilities. Participation in Crown Court or adult Magistrates' Courts is particularly problematic and, arguably, all hearings involving children and young people should be held in Youth Courts to ensure that they can participate effectively, are not subject to the secondary harm caused by inappropriate court proceedings, and receive appropriate sentencing or remand decisions. Children and young people appearing in the Youth Court also have greater protection of their anonymity, at least whilst they are aged under 18, and these provisions should be automatically extended to those appearing in the Crown Court. It is also imperative that this protection should continue even when a child turns 18.

There are concerns about the relatively high number of children and young people who are remanded to youth detention accommodation (see Chapter 5) and there is a need for the greater provision of alternatives, such as remand foster care (Lipscombe, 2006), particularly when the impact on sentencing is considered. The failings in PSRs raised by HM Inspectorate of Probation and others (2011) need to be addressed due to the impact the PSR may have on the sentence received, although, as discussed in the next chapter, courts do not necessarily follow the recommendations made within the PSR. The following chapter considers the community sentences available to the court, before a consideration of the use of custody is presented in Chapter 5.

Further reading

CPS (undated) *Legal Guidance: Youth Offenders* provides further detail on trial procedures, including specific issues for young defendants with learning disabilities or impairments, determining venue/jurisdiction.

HM Court Service/YJB (2010) *Making it Count in Court* – a practice guide, jointly produced by Her Majesty's Court Service and the YJB, which includes guidance on the preparation of reports, YOTs role in court, presentation in court and post-court administration.

HM Inspectorate of Probation, HM Inspectorate of Courts Administration and HM Crown Prosecution Service Inspectorate (2011) *Not Making Enough Difference: A Joint Inspection of Youth Offending Court Work and Reports* provides a critical analysis of the work of YOTs in courts and report-writing, highlighting failings and weaknesses as well as good practice examples.

Lipscombe, J (2006) *Care or Control? Foster Care for Young People on Remand* – a research study on the use of foster care for children and young people on remand; also includes a comprehensive review of the development of remand legislation.

Prison Reform Trust (2009) *Vulnerable Defendants in the Criminal Courts: A Review of Provision for Adults and Children* – provides a review of the additional measures needed to support children and young people appearing in court.

The Advocates Gateway www.theadvocatesgateway.org contains free toolkits and guidance aimed at helping advocates and the bench – subjects covered include: ground rules hearings; autism spectrum disorder; learning disability; specific language impairment; dyspraxia and other disabilities; children and young people; those under seven and those functioning at a very young age.

4

COMMUNITY SENTENCES

AT A GLANCE THIS CHAPTER COVERS:

- the scaled approach and sentencing
- restorative justice
- community sentences
- additional sentences and arrangements
- enforcement and breach of orders

This chapter considers the community sentences available for children and young people convicted of a criminal offence in either the Youth Court or the Crown Court. Custodial sentences for more serious and/or more persistent offenders are discussed in Chapter 5. The purpose of sentencing is set out in the CJIA 2008: courts must have regard to the principal aim of the youth justice system, which is to prevent offending and reoffending (s. 9(2)(a)) (see Introduction). Courts must also have regard to the welfare of the offenders in accordance with s. 44 CYPA 1933 and, in addition, should take account of the following purposes of sentencing (s. 9(3)):

- the punishment of offenders;
- the reform and rehabilitation of offenders;
- the protection of the public; and
- the making of reparation by offenders to persons affected by their offences.

The Supreme Court has commented, in relation to children and young people, that a key aim 'of any sentence imposed should be to promote the process of maturation, the development of a sense of responsibility, and the growth of a healthy adult personality and identity' (*R v Secretary of State, ex parte Maria Smith* [2005], Baroness Hale at para. 25). This is reiterated in para. 1.3 of the guidelines for sentencing young people, issued by the Sentencing Guidelines Council (SGC) (now the Sentencing Council) in 2009, which states that 'the intention [of sentencing] is to establish responsibility and, at the same time, to promote re-integration rather than to impose retribution'.

This conflation of the different purposes of sentencing presents a number of problems for those in the youth justice system (Baker, 2009): different aims can require contradictory actions and it is almost inevitable that one aim will have to take precedence over another. This is a reflection (and perhaps a result) of the inherent tensions between the different aims of the youth justice system, discussed in the Introduction. While the Sentencing Council establishes the general principles of sentencing practice for both adults and children, the PSR written by the YOT (Chapter 3) should provide the court with guidance as to which sentence is most appropriate for the individual young person, considering both the need to prevent offending and the welfare of the child. The recommendations of the PSR do not have to be followed by the sentencing magistrate/judge and this has led to a number of appeals. For example,

R v Maughan (Donna) and Others [2012] held that an appeal against sentencing should be allowed as a custodial sentence was deemed excessive and that insufficient weight was given to the welfare of the child. Conversely, some appeals are not allowed/held, based on the view that the nature of the offence warranted a harsher sentence (for instance, *R v K (A N)* [2014]).

Arguably, youthfulness is seen as a mitigating factor in sentencing and research shows that young offenders are generally sentenced less harshly than adults who have committed similar offences (Flood-Page and Mackie, 1998, cited by Cavadino et al., 2013) – but it is important to note that this is not always the case and some sentences for children and young people are more intrusive/lengthy than adults would receive. Article 37 UNCRC emphasizes the need to provide a range of disposals for children involved in offending behaviour – including care, probation, guidance, foster care and educational and vocational training – and that detention must be a measure of last resort.

The scaled approach and sentencing

As discussed in Chapter 1, the YJB introduced the scaled approach to sentencing, based on the idea of a single generic community sentence for young offenders, with a range of interventions, escalating in intensiveness if a young person continues to offend (first mooted in *Every Child Matters* (DCSF, 2003) and the accompanying document, *Youth Justice: The Next Steps* (Home Office, 2003)). The scaled approach is underpinned by the principle that sentencing should be guided by the aim of preventing offending by tailoring the sentence towards the needs of the offender, rather than in response to the offence committed. The level of intervention necessary should be assessed and delivered in accordance with the risk, needs and responsivity framework (but see the criticisms of risk-based assessments in Chapter 1). The rigidity of the scaled approach to sentencing has been criticized for restricting the ability of professionals to use their judgement, for example, by reducing the impact of mitigating factors or limiting opportunities for sentencing interventions to reward a young person's successful achievements (Fox and Arnull, 2013). Furthermore, due to the competing requirements of sentencing, the scaled approach only really becomes applicable where interventions can be dissociated from specific court orders and where the local judiciary support the work of the YOT when sentencing young people (McConnochie, 2009).

On-the-spot questions

1 What factors need to be considered by the judiciary when determining sentence?
2 How may balancing these factors affect sentencing consistency?

Restorative justice

The responsibilization agenda (see Introduction) is underpinned by a philosophy of restorative justice and all sentencing disposals now allow the opportunity for restorative interventions. The Green Paper *Breaking the Cycle* (MoJ, 2010) details the Coalition government's aim to increase the use of restorative justice, from early intervention and prevention activities through to behaviour management strategies within the secure estate (Fox and Arnull, 2013; Staines, 2013). The Crime and Courts Act 2013 contains provisions which allow courts to defer passing sentence while imposing on the offender a requirement that they participate in restorative justice activities. This will require the consent of the offender and of any other persons, such as victims, who would also participate.

Restorative justice is a contested concept but, broadly, restorative approaches aim to allow an offender to make amends for the wrongdoing or harm they have caused and, in doing so, restore the victim's faith in society (Johnstone and Van Ness, 2007). The justice process is seen as belonging to the community, not the state, with the victim being placed at the heart of the process. A restorative intervention is essentially a process whereby any parties involved in or affected by unwanted behaviour resolve collectively how to deal with the aftermath of the incident(s) and its implications for the future. There is considerable overlap between reparation and restorative justice, but they are not the same: restorative justice involves communication between the parties affected; reparation involves the redress of balance between parties involved through a person's actions. Whilst reparation can be ordered by a court without any communication between the parties, restorative justice involves communication, which may result in a party agreeing to make reparation. Reparation involves the offender making practical amends to repair the harm caused by the offence. This may include a verbal or written apology, direct activity-based reparation to the victim (such as repairing damage caused to property or undertaking other practical tasks), or through indirect reparation (constructive work to help the local community). The victim is usually consulted about what form they would like the repara-tion to take, although their wishes need to be balanced against the avail-ability of suitable activities, appropriate supervision and health and safety requirements.

The implementation of restorative justice within the youth justice system has attracted criticism, including the potential for net-widening and the erosion of legal rights (for example, where an out-of-court restorative disposal is implemented, see Chapter 3; or where a referral order is passed, see below), and the potential for re-victimization of the victim (Fox and Arnull, 2013). It is also difficult to evaluate the benefits of restorative justice as some argue that participation in the process is sufficient while others believe that the achievement of a specified outcome is necessary for the intervention to be deemed successful (Walgrave, 2000). Associated with this are questions about the use of coercion: central to purist restorative approaches is the empowerment of both victims and offenders and the voluntary nature of any involvement in the processes. This is questionable within formalized justice systems, where a young person's involvement in restorative or reparative interven-tions may be a required element of their sentence and elements of coer-cion may be apparent, for example, if an agreement is not met, the young person may be referred back to court for alternative sentencing (Shapland et al., 2006; Moore and Mitchell, 2009). The implementation of restorative justice is not uniform nationally and there are concerns that financial pressures could lead to further inconsistency, both in availabil-ity of restorative alternatives and the integrity of the measures adopted.

Community sentences

Sentences available for children and young people range from an absolute discharge through to long-term detention (Chapter 5). MoJ statistics show that 29,343 community sentences and 11,478 first-tier sentences (discharges, fines, otherwise dealt with disposals) were passed in 2012/2013, reflecting a continued decrease in the numbers of young people sentenced over the last 10 years (MoJ, 2014).

Absolute/conditional discharges – these can be passed where the offending is deemed to fall below the level of seriousness required for a community sentence. An absolute discharge imposes no penalty; reflect-ing the court's view that, although a finding of guilt was technically necessary, the child was morally blameless or the offence was very trivial. A conditional discharge imposes no penalty as long as no further offences are committed within a stipulated period (from 6 months to 3 years). If the terms of a conditional discharge are breached, the child will be re-sentenced for the original and subsequent offences. A discharge does not preclude the court from issuing a compensation order or an order for costs on either the young person or their parents. Prior to 1998, a conditional discharge was the most common first-tier disposal for young people. Under s. 66 of the CDA 1998, their use was limited (conditional discharges were made unavailable if the young person had received a final warning in the previous 2 years, unless there were exceptional circumstances) and so declined (Cavadino et al., 2013). LASPO 2012, however, has made further amendments such that a court may impose a conditional or absolute discharge on a young person who pleads guilty to their first offence as an alternative to a referral order (see below), which may lead to a subsequent increase in the use of discharges.

Fines – a court may impose a fine for an offence that must reflect the seriousness of the offence, taking into account any mitigating or aggravating factors, and the personal and financial circumstances of the person ordered to pay the fine. Under s. 135 PCC(S)A 2000, Youth Courts can imposed a maximum of £250 for those aged 10–13 and £1000 for those aged 14–17. There is no maximum fine in the Crown Court unless it is hearing an appeal against a sentence imposed by a lower court. If the child is under 16, the parent/guardian will be expected to pay the fine unless the court considers this to be unreasonable. If the child is 16 or 17, the court will use its discretion over who should pay. Although the fine may be paid immediately, the court will generally specify a time period over which the fine must be paid by instalments.

Compensation orders – these are designed to compensate the victim of an offence for personal injury, loss or damage arising from the offence. A child may be ordered to pay compensation, either as a standalone penalty or in addition to another order. As with fines, a parent or guardian will be ordered to pay on behalf of those under 16, and the court will use its discretion for 16 or 17-year-olds; the court must take into account the financial circumstances of the person being ordered to pay. The maximum amount that can be ordered is £5000 for each offence; it can be paid immediately or within a specified time period. The court should only award compensation in simple and clear-cut cases, not when calculation is not straightforward (for example, where the extent of injury or cost of repairs is not clear). At the same time, there is a presumption that the courts will impose compensation wherever appropriate and must give reasons for not making an order.

On-the-spot question	What are the implications of fines and compensation orders for children and their parent(s)?

Reparation orders – introduced by the CDA 1998, a young person can be ordered to make reparation either to the victim (with their consent) or to the wider community. While the court is supposed to specify the nature of reparation, in practice, the YOT will be involved in assessing and advising what may be appropriate and in facilitating and monitoring the reparative activity. Reparation must be proportionate to the offence, may not exceed 24 hours' duration and the order may last a maximum of 3 months. The court is required to give reasons for not imposing such an order where it has the power to do so but, in practice, the use of reparation orders has declined since the introduction of the referral order, with only 453 being made in 2012/2013, fewer than half the number made in the previous year (MoJ, 2014, supplementary tables).

Referral orders – the referral order system was established by the YJCE 1999 and was implemented nationwide in 2002. Section 16 PCC(S)A 2000 required the Youth Court to make a referral order for first-time offenders who plead guilty, and ss 35–57 CJA 2008 extended the provisions to those previously subject to referral orders in certain circumstances.

Under s. 16(1) PCC(S)A 2000 a referral order cannot be given to a young person where:

- the sentence is fixed by law (such as in cases of murder);
- the offence is so serious that the court proposes to impose a custodial sentence;
- the court is proposing to make a hospital order;
- the offence is relatively minor and the court proposes to give an absolute or a conditional discharge.

Subject to those exceptions, the circumstances in which a referral order must be imposed are where:

- the offender (aged 10–17) pleads guilty to the offence and any connected offence;
- and referral is available to the court; and
- the offence is punishable with imprisonment; and
- the offender has not previously been convicted of an offence.

As noted above, LASPO 2012 has made further amendments such that a court may impose a conditional or absolute discharge on a young person who pleads guilty to their first offence as an alternative to a referral order, and has removed the restriction on repeated use, allowing the courts to make a referral order whenever they consider it suitable.

The referral order is based on the principles of restorative justice and diverts the offender from the court to a Youth Offender Panel (YOP). The YOP (consisting of one YOT member and two lay volunteers) is less formal than the court and aims to discuss with the young person and their family the reasons for their behaviour, what steps can be taken to repair the harm caused and what is needed to prevent further offences (Johns, 2011). Since April 2013, YOT panel advisers and panel members have been trained in restorative justice conference facilitation training, prior to participation in panels. The victim should be invited to attend the meeting, or to participate indirectly if they wish. The purpose of the panel is to negotiate a youth offender contract that includes reparation and elements aimed at preventing further offending (Cavadino et al., 2013); the duration of the contract (between 3 and 12 months) is determined by the court based on the seriousness of the offence. The involvement of social workers here is important in terms of assessment and putting into effect the panel's decision, but the professional role remains advisory and the YOT members do not participate in decision-making (Johns, 2011). If no agreement can be reached, or the contract is later breached, the case will be referred back to the court for alternative sentencing. Referral orders differ from other community sentences in that the content of the intervention is determined by the YOP and the provisions for enforcement are accordingly amended to allow the panel to determine whether a failure to comply is sufficiently serious to warrant a return to court. In the event of breach proceedings, the court can allow the contract to continue or revoke the referral order and re-sentence for the original offence.

In 2012/2013, 15,248 young people were sentenced to a referral order, just over a third of all those sentenced by the courts – although the number has decreased since a peak of 31,597 in 2007/2008 (MoJ, 2014, supplementary tables).

The YOP has similarities to the Scottish Children's Hearings System (Pickford and Dugmore, 2012), adopting a potentially more holistic stance towards young offending. However, there are a range of problematic tensions within the use of referral orders and YOPs, for instance: there are often low levels of victim involvement (Earle, 2005); the young person is not entitled to legal representation and there are no due process requirements, meaning that a young person's legal rights may not be upheld; the use of the term 'contract' implies negotiation, yet the young person is essentially compelled to agree or they will be referred back to court for non-compliance (Pickford, 2000); no appeal against the contract is allowed; and the sentence – a minimum of 3 months – may be longer and more intrusive than sentences adults receive for similar offences. Furthermore, the panels may not be socially representative of the area (Crawford and Newburn, 2002) and the variation in the composition, structures and procedures of the panels can result in inconsistent, non-standardized 'justice' (Crawford and Newburn, 2003). The reliance on volunteers also sits somewhat uncomfortably within the context of professionalization, standardization and evidence-based practice otherwise promoted by the YJB (Crawford and Newburn, 2003).

| *On-the-spot question* | What are the benefits and disadvantages of restorative approaches, including reparation orders and referral orders? |

Youth rehabilitation orders

Youth rehabilitation orders (YROs) were introduced by s. 148 CJIA 2008, replacing the range of community sentences previously available, and can be imposed where offences are 'serious enough' to merit them. A YRO can last for a maximum of 3 years; normally a young person can only be subject to one YRO at any one time, so a new YRO can only be imposed if the existing order is revoked by the court. The content of the YRO is drawn from the elements listed below, within the rules that disallow certain combinations and ensure that overall maxima are not exceeded (YJB, 2010b). Reflecting the complex aims and philosophies of the youth justice system, the different elements have been variously designed to provide for punishment, protection of the public, reducing reoffending, rehabilitation and reparation:

- activity requirement;
- local authority residence requirement;
- attendance centre requirement;
- mental health treatment requirement;
- curfew requirement;
- programme requirement;
- drug-testing requirement;
- prohibited activity requirement;
- drug treatment requirement;
- residence requirement;
- education requirement;
- supervision requirement;
- electronic-monitoring requirement;
- unpaid work requirement;
- exclusion requirement;
- intoxicating substance treatment requirement;
- YRO with intensive fostering (IF);
- YRO with intensive supervision and surveillance (ISS).

Not all requirements are available throughout England and Wales, so there will be some variation in the requirements attached to YROs. The requirements last the full duration of the YRO unless the court stipulates otherwise. Some requirements need the consent of the young person, for example, a mental health treatment requirement, drug treatment requirement or an intoxicating substance requirement should only be used where the young person has not agreed to a voluntary referral but has expressed willingness to comply with the requirement. Furthermore, there are particular requisites for some requirements; for instance, an intoxicating substance requirement cannot be included unless the court is satisfied, based upon an assessment undertaken by a specialist substance misuse worker that a) the offender is dependent on, or has a propensity to misuse, an intoxicating substance and b) that the offender's dependency or propensity is such as requires and may be susceptible to treatment. If a young person does not meet the intervention threshold required by the CJIA 2008 or does not agree to the requirement being made, interventions to educate the young person about their substance use could (and perhaps should) be included as part of an activity, supervision or programme requirement.

There are particular combinations of requirements that must/must not run concurrently with others (for example, the drug-testing requirement has to be run alongside a drug treatment requirement). IF and ISS can only be required if the offence is imprisonable and so serious that a custodial sentence would have been used were these requirements not available. ISS and IF are also deemed incompatible and cannot run alongside each other. ISS must be considered by a court as part of the scaled approach for all young people at risk of custody; the court does not have to consult the YOT regarding the suitability of the sentence. A YRO with ISS or an IF requirement must be for a minimum of 6 months; the ISS requirement must be a minimum of 90 days and a maximum of 180 days.

ISS is based upon the intensive supervision and surveillance programmes that were introduced in 2001, acknowledging that custody could not, and did not, meet the needs of high-risk young offenders (Arnull et al., 2005; Fox and Arnull, 2013). The ISS requirement can have reparative elements, seek to address criminogenic factors and work with the young person to put structures in place (interpersonal skills development, family support and so forth) to encourage desistance. As noted in Chapter 3, ISS can also be used pre-sentence/conviction as a condition of bail and post-conviction as a condition of a notice of supervision on release from custody. There are three bands of ISS (1 – high intensity; 2 – medium intensity; 3 – extended ISS), which incorporate different levels of contact and electronic-monitoring arrangements (YJB, *National Standards*, 2013a). For example, on a 6-month sentence, the most intensive level of ISS has 25 hours' contact per week in the first 3 months, with 5 hours per week for a further 3 months; on a 12-month programme a level one ISS would require 25 hours' contact for 4 months, resulting in over 2500 contact hours over the year – which may be significantly more intensive and intrusive than the sentence given to an adult for an equivalent offence.

IF was introduced in the CJIA 2008 as alternative to custody and can form part of a YRO for young people 'whose home life is felt to have contributed significantly to their offending behaviour' (YJB, 2010a:84). A young person can remain in an IF placement for up to 12 months; a programme of support can simultaneously be offered to their family, including family therapy, counselling and parenting skills. IF placements are based on the highly structured Multi-Dimensional Treatment Foster Care model, which originated in Oregon in the 1980s (Fisher and Chamberlain, 2000), but their availability nationwide is extremely limited.

In 2012/2013, 13,527 YROs were given to young people, a decrease of almost a quarter (24 per cent) from the previous year (MoJ, 2014); in 2011/2012 less than a third (29 per cent) of YROs included only one requirement, with nearly a third (32 per cent) having two requirements; 4 per cent had five or more requirements (MoJ, 2013a). The most commonly used requirement is supervision (used in 36 per cent of YRO requirements); other common requirements included curfew orders (15 per cent), electronic monitoring (12 per cent), unpaid work (7 per cent) and attendance centre orders (4 per cent) (MoJ, 2014).

The YRO has benefits for young people and the courts, simplifying the sentencing structure and allowing a bespoke package of interventions to address individual needs and risks (MoJ, 2013a), but has also faced criticism as being a 'smorgasbord' of options with no coherent or rational basis, developed in the hope that something will work (Pickford and Dugmore, 2012). As noted above, the interventions should be delivered in accordance with the risk, needs and responsivity assessments within the framework of the scaled approach but, in practice, interventions may be selected based on what is available in the locality, not what is needed, especially for girls (Arnull and Eagle, 2009). Concerns have been raised about the potential risk of 'up-tariffing', as there is now a shorter 'ladder'

PRACTICE FOCUS

Janine, aged 15, has been convicted of causing actual bodily harm, having kicked and punched another girl who was admitted to hospital for observation and required five sutures. At the time of the offence, Janine admits to having been 'very drunk'; she drinks alcohol every evening and her parents feel she is 'addicted' to alcohol. Janine has a record of previous offences of violence and often goes out with the expressed intention of becoming drunk.

- What principles need to be taken into consideration when deciding which sentence to pass?
- Why would a referral order not be appropriate in this instance?
- What requirements could be attached to a YRO?
- What would be necessary to enable an intoxicating substance requirement to be attached to a YRO?

of community sentences for courts to consider before a custodial sentence appears appropriate (Baker, 2009).

Additional orders and arrangements

Multi-Agency Public Protection Arrangements

The CJA 2003 provides for the establishment of MAPPA, requiring local criminal justice agencies and other bodies to work together in managing the risks to the public of serious harm by those convicted of sexual or violent offences. The MAPPA responsible authority includes the police, probation and the prison services and has a statutory duty to establish arrangements for the assessment and management of risk presented by specified sexual and violent offenders. In addition, a range of other agencies are under a duty to cooperate with the responsible authority, including YOTs, social/children's services, local housing authorities, local education authorities and NHS trusts and strategic health authorities.

Some young people will be subject to the multi-disciplinary surveillance of MAPPA, either because the nature of the offence they have committed (for example, violent or sexual offences as set out in Schedule 15 CJA 2003, or prolific offending) is such as to mean that they must be referred (categories 1 and 2) or because the practitioner's concerns about the risk they pose are such as to warrant referral (category 3). The MAPPA must give consideration to the responsibility to safeguard and promote the welfare of children (Children Act 2004) as well as the risk of harm the young offender presents to others. Children's services should always be represented at these MAPPA meetings – the YOT officer should not be seen as representing the local authority. The YOT is responsible for identifying which of its cases are MAPPA cases within 3 days of sentence.

Category 1 cases (likely to be in the majority) are subject to ordinary agency management, such that the YOT will work with the young person following its relevant policy, procedures and standards. Category 2 and 3 cases are subject to a MAPPA meeting to identify the risks present and to devise an effective MAPPA risk management plan to mitigate those risks. The MAPPA should also consider the disclosure of information, including the risk of harm to the child or young person that could occur because disclosure has taken place and whether the LSCB should be informed if disclosure is made (MoJ/National Offender Management Service (NOMS)/MAPPA, 2012).

MAPPA is essentially adult-centric (Baker, 2009) but is applied to young people equally, which raises questions about how well it addresses the particular risks and needs presented by children and young people. Furthermore, it is difficult to assess risk accurately (Fox and Arnull, 2013; see also Chapter 1) and some young people may become subject to potentially intrusive multi-disciplinary surveillance that may be unwarranted.

Orders imposed on parents

Parents can be ordered to pay fines and compensation orders for their children, but also can be subject to the following provisions.

Parental bind-over – parents undertake to exercise proper care and control to ensure that the young person complies with community sentences and to prevent the young person committing further offences. The parent(s) can be required to pay up to £1000 if there are further offences or failure to comply with the requirements of community sentences (s. 150 PCC(S)A 2000).

Parenting orders – s. 324 CJA 2003 allows a parenting order to run alongside a referral order where this is appropriate or, as detailed in Chapter 1, where a young person is found guilty of anti-social behaviour (CDA 1998). The parent(s) is expected to attend counselling or guidance sessions, to improve their parenting skills; they are also expected to exercise a measure of control over their child (for example, ensuring they attend school). Failure to comply with a parenting order is a criminal offence punishable with a fine of up to £1000.

Additional orders

There is also an increasing number of civil orders under different legislative Acts, which can be passed against children and young people post-conviction, including (but not limited to) IPNAs (see Chapter 1), sexual offences prevention orders, restraining orders, football spectator banning orders, travel restriction orders and non-molestation orders. These orders are procedurally civil so lack the additional safeguards associated with criminal procedures but breach of the orders is a criminal offence that can result in severe sanctions (see Ashworth and Redmayne, 2010, for a more detailed discussion of these orders). Courts can also make a hospital order, under s. 37 Mental Health Act (MHA) 1983 (as amended by s. 4(5) Mental Health Act 2007) where a child or young person is convicted of an offence punishable with imprisonment, other than murder, or is found unfit to plead but to have committed the offence in court proceedings.

In order to make a hospital order the court must be satisfied on the written or oral evidence of two doctors, at least one of whom must be approved under s. 12 MHA 1983, that the young person is suffering from a mental disorder which makes it appropriate for them to be detained in hospital for medical treatment and that appropriate medical treatment is available within 28 days of the order. Where the Crown Court makes a hospital order it may also make a restriction order under s. 41 MHA 1983, which restricts the patient's discharge, transfer or leave of absence from hospital without the consent of the Secretary of State. The Magistrates' Court has no power to make a restriction order, but where it has convicted a person aged 14 years or more of an offence punishable on summary conviction with imprisonment and it considers that a hospital order and restriction order should be made, it can commit the young person to the Crown Court to be dealt with for the offence (s. 43 MHA 1983).

Enforcement and breach of orders

YOTs have the responsibility of ensuring that children cooperate with any court-ordered community-based intervention, within the framework established by the *National Standards* (YJB, 2013c). Where attempts to encourage compliance are unsuccessful, the YOT can, in appropriate cases, initiate breach action which involves returning the young person to court. The *National Standards* contain a generic enforcement procedure that governs the majority of court sentences, including the community element of a DTO (Chapter 5). There are three stages:

- if there is an apparent failure to attend, the YOT must seek an explanation from the child within 1 working day and then determine whether to record the absence as acceptable or unacceptable;
- an unacceptable failure to comply must result in the issue of a formal written warning;
- when there is a further unacceptable failure to comply once two warnings have been given, breach action will normally be initiated within 5 working days, but there is discretion in exceptional cases for the YOT manager to determine that a return to court is not appropriate at that stage.

The powers of the court in relation to breach vary according to the nature of the original order but include taking no action, imposing a fine to ensure the child's future compliance, or revoking the original order and re-sentencing for the original offence, taking into account the extent of compliance. In such circumstances, the court can impose any order that would have been available at the original sentence hearing. *Breaking the Cycle* (MoJ, 2010) suggested that YOTs introduce 'compliance panels' to ensure that court orders are enforced more consistently and efficiently.

Conclusions

Whilst discretion in sentencing is necessary to allow the individual circumstances of an offence and the needs and characteristics of the young person to be taken into consideration, it can lead to differential treatment and inconsistencies in sentencing. Sentencing guidance is just guidance and sentencers have to balance a number of potentially competing principles – the punishment of offenders, the reduction of crime, the reform and rehabilitation of offenders, the protection of the public, and the making of reparation, plus, for children and young people, the welfare of the child. The difficulties in achieving such a balance within the requisite legislation are apparent within the number of appeals against sentencing heard in the appeals courts. The appropriateness of some sentences for children and young people may be questionable: for example, placing the responsibility for paying fines or compensation orders made against children under 16 with their parents may either effectively devolve the punishment to the parents and absolve the child of responsibility, or conversely lead to greater punishment by the parents who resent the imposition of a fine. Restorative justice approaches are generally seen as a more progressive response to youth offending but there is a need to ensure that legal safeguards are applied and monitored to ensure that the requirements of the order are proportionate to the harm caused and are no more intrusive than sentences for adults who have committed equivalent offences. The rigidity of the YRO and its potential for rapid up-tariffing has been criticized, although it does aim to provide a more tailored response to children and young people's individual needs and can provide a robust alternative to custodial sentences. The following chapter considers the use of custodial sentences for children and young people, for whom community sentences are deemed inappropriate.

Further reading

Johnstone G and D W Van Ness (eds) (2007) *Handbook of Restorative Justice* provides a comprehensive and accessible overview of the key concepts and principles of restorative justice, the development of different restorative justice practices, and key tensions and issues within the restorative justice movement.

MoJ/YJB (2012) *Referral Order Guidance* provides detailed information about the referral order, the recruitment and role of panel members, the negotiation of contracts and measures to address compliance.

SGC (2009) *Overarching Principles: Sentencing Youths – Definitive Guide* is an essential reference for practitioners within youth justice; it establishes the general principles of sentencing practice, sets out specific guidance criteria for particular sentences, and gives advice in relation to the responsibilities of parents/guardians.

YJB (2010a) *A Report on the Intensive Fostering Pilot Programme* summarizes longitudinal research into IF by staff at the University of York, London School of Economics and the University of Manchester, highlighting the strengths and difficulties of IF. Overall, the study concludes that IF may be a better alternative to custody and should continue to be implemented.

YJB (2010b) *The Youth Rehabilitation Order and Other Youth Justice Provisions of the Criminal Justice and Immigration Act 2008 (B422): Practice Guidance for Youth Offending Teams* provides non-statutory guidance for the CJIA 2008, outlining the YRO, including specific detail on each of the requirements, and practice implications.

5

CUSTODIAL SENTENCES

AT A GLANCE THIS CHAPTER COVERS:

- overarching sentencing principles for custodial sentences
- custodial sentences
- the juvenile secure estate
- concerns and breaches of rights within custody
- determining release dates
- licence and supervision
- parole
- resettlement
- criminal records

The influence of popular punitivism in the 1990s led to England and Wales having one of the highest rates of child incarceration in Western Europe, despite arguably lower rates of offending behaviour (Junger-Tas et al., 1994; Gould and Payne, 2004). However, significant reductions in the child custodial population (those aged under 18) have been achieved recently, partly as a result of the impact of early intervention, prevention and diversionary programmes on the number of children and young people appearing at court (Chapter 1) and other changes in sentencing practice, such as the introduction of the YRO (Chapter 4). The average custodial population of under-18s has reduced by approximately 60 per cent from over 3000 in 2008 to 1544 in 2012/2013 (1708 if 18-year-olds held in the youth secure estate are included) (MoJ, 2014). However, the average custody rate (the proportion of sentences passed in court that are custodial) has remained relatively static over the last decade and was 6.4 per cent in 2012/2013; furthermore the average length of time spent in custody on a DTO has increased from 106 days in 2008/2009 to 115 days in 2012/2013 (MoJ, 2014). This may reflect changes in the population of young people appearing before the courts: as early intervention and prevention programmes and diversionary schemes divert young people from the courts, those who do come before the courts may have a greater history of offending and so receive harsher penalties (MoJ, 2013a); or it may reflect increasingly punitive attitudes towards those receiving custodial sentences.

Notwithstanding the reduction in the child custody population, the incarceration of children remains particularly concerning when the troubled and disadvantaged backgrounds of these children are considered and in light of the serious concerns repeatedly raised about custodial institutions for young people (Cavadino et al., 2013). Many commentators, including the YJB itself (YJB, 2011; also Cavadino et al., 2013; Fox and Arnull, 2013), have questioned the effectiveness of imprisonment, noting that reoffending rates remain high, particularly for children and young people, and that there are some sentenced to custody for whom a community sentence would be more appropriate. This chapter discusses the range of custodial sentences available for children and young people, including DTOs and s. 90/s. 91 sentences (PCC(S)A 2000) and other extended sentences. The chapter will then consider the experience of custody and highlight some of the breaches of children's rights that currently occur, before detailing the process of parole, release and resettlement.

Overarching sentencing principles for custodial sentences

The SGC's guidance *Overarching Principles: Sentencing Youth* (2009) establishes the core principles that should be considered when sentencing children (see also Chapter 4) and which are particularly important when sentencing children to periods of detention. It is a generalizable principle that custodial sentences must only be exercised as a last resort:

s. 152

2 The court must not pass a custodial sentence unless it is of the opinion that the offence, or the combination of the offence and one or more offences associated with it, was so serious that neither a fine alone nor a community sentence can be justified for the offence.

CJA 2003

Paragraph 11.5 SGC guidance (2009) recognizes the relevance of international agreements such as the UNCRC to the approach to be adopted by a court in sentencing. Article 37(b) UNCRC provides that: 'The arrest, detention or imprisonment of a child shall be … used as a measure of last resort and for the shortest appropriate period of time.' Similarly, rule 17.1(b) Beijing Rules 1985 stipulates that restrictions on the personal liberty of juveniles shall be limited to the minimum possible. This has been incorporated into domestic law under s. 152(3) CJA 2003, which states that custody should be for the shortest time commensurate with the seriousness of the offence. While this provision applies equally to adults, the SGC guidelines state that 'there is an expectation that generally a young person will be dealt with less severely than an adult offender' (para. 3.1). Depending on the maturity of the young person, detention usually should have a starting point of half to three-quarters of that for an adult offender (SGC, 2009).

The welfare principle

As with any action made by courts, s. 44(1) CYPA 1933 requires sentencing courts to have regard to the young person's welfare (see Chapter 4); this is reiterated in Article 3 UNCRC, which stipulates that the 'best interests of the child shall be a primary consideration in all actions concerning children' (although there is considerable debate over how to determine what is in a child's 'best interests'). The Supreme Court held that the spirit of the best interests principle has been translated into domestic legislation through the Children Act 2004 (Howard League,

2012) but, as discussed in Chapter 4, a number of appeals have challenged the apparent failure to apply the welfare principle in sentencing decisions, particularly where custodial sentences have been passed.

There is a growing body of case law confirming that the welfare principle requires a holistic approach to be taken in determining sentence length (see, for example, Lord Woolf's actions in reducing the minimum term for Thompson and Venables in the key case analysis, below; see also Howard League, 2010). Reducing the length of a sentence for a child by an arbitrary amount would be considered insufficient, as it would be equivalent to treating the fact that the defendant was a child as a mitigating factor, rather than actively considering the child's welfare, as required by the CYPA 1933 (Howard League, 2010). Paragraph 4 SGC guidelines (2009) identifies a number of factors that are relevant to the application of the welfare principle, including the high risk of self-harm and suicide affecting young people in custody and the high incidence of mental illness and learning difficulties among young people receiving custodial sentences (discussed further below).

Custodial sentences

Detention and training orders

DTOs were created under the CDA 1998 and are the most common form of custodial sentence given to children aged 12–17 years: in 2012/2013 58 per cent of the average population of young people in custody was serving a DTO (MoJ, 2014). DTOs can be imposed by Magistrates' Courts or Crown Courts, for a period of between 4 and 24 months, if the court is of the opinion that the offence(s) is so serious that a community sentence cannot be justified. For offenders aged 12–14, the court must also deem the young person to be a persistent young offender (s. 100 PCC(S)A 2000). The first half of a DTO is served in custody, the second half is spent on licence in the community, under the supervision of the YOT. As discussed in Chapter 4, the sentencing structure within the scaled approach retained ISS as one of the 'pick and mix' options that can be added to YROs. The court, when passing a custodial sentence, must thus state that a YRO with an ISS or IF provision is not appropriate and the reasons why, in addition to meeting the existing criteria for custodial sentences; ISS or IF can be a condition of the community licence period of the DTO under a notice of supervision.

Additional custodial sentences

Further custodial sentences are available to the Crown Court for children and young people who are convicted of grave offences. Children and young people convicted of murder are subject to a mandatory indeterminate sentence of long-term detention known as 'detention at Her Majesty's pleasure' or 's. 90'; for other serious offences a specified period of long-term detention may be imposed under s. 91 PCC(S)A 2000, subject to the same maximum lengths as in the case of adults.

Section 90 PCC(S)A 2000

Section 90 PCC(S)A 2000 specifies that where a child under the age of 18 at the time the offence was committed is convicted of murder, the court shall sentence him/her to be detained during Her Majesty's pleasure; this is a mandatory sentence and the only sentence available to the court for children convicted of murder. A minimum period of detention is specified in the tariff set by the court (under the Criminal Justice and Court Services Act 2000), to mark the requirements of punishment and deterrence. Once the minimum term has expired, the young person will remain in custody until the Parole Board considers it safe to release them into the community. The Parole Board can deny release, thereby keeping the child in prison beyond the minimum term of imprisonment if they are still considered to be a risk to the public (discussed later). Until November 2000 the tariff was set by the Home Secretary, but this was found to be in breach of Article 6 ECHR, on the grounds that the Home Secretary could not be considered an independent tribunal. When deemed appropriate by the Parole Board, the young person will be released on licence for life and can be recalled for any breach of their licence.

The minimum and maximum terms of detention under s. 90 for a child or young person differ from those applicable to adults sentenced for murder: the CJA 2003 requires the court to have regard to a 'starting point' of 12 years in determining the minimum term to be served in custody by a child or young person, as opposed to 15 years for adults. Children and young people aged under 21 cannot be sentenced to 'whole life orders', which have been applied to adults (although such sentences are the subject of current human rights debates).

Section 90 sentences have been recognized by the House of Lords to be unique sentences that require the promotion of the child's welfare

(Howard League, 2010); as such it is the policy of the MoJ to allow for the minimum term ordered to be reviewed in light of the progress and development made by the young person once they have served half of the original minimum term.

→ KEY CASE ANALYSIS ←

V, T v UK **[2000] and** *Re Thompson (Tariff Recommendation)* **[2001]: sentencing children and young people to long-term detention**

The most notorious case involving children sentenced to long-term detention is perhaps the killing of James Bulger by Robert Thompson and Jon Venables in 1993. As well as attracting wide-ranging and long-lasting media attention, this case has arguably influenced the youth justice system more than any other, with a number of legislative changes directly or indirectly following from this case (such as the abolition of *doli incapax*, see Introduction; and the Practice Direction regarding the trial of children and young people in the Crown Court, see Chapter 3). The 8-year sentence tariff set by the trial judge was increased to 10 years by Lord Chief Justice Lord Taylor of Gosforth and was then increased again to 15 years by the Home Secretary, largely as a result of public pressure. This was later found unlawful by the Law Lords who ruled that the Home Secretary had acted illegally in raising the boys' tariff. In *V, T v UK* [2000], it was argued that the automatic imposition of a sentence of detention at Her Majesty's pleasure amounted to inhuman and degrading treatment under Article 3 ECHR and the value of the purpose of the sentence in terms of deterrence and punishment in the case of a very young child was questioned. However, the court rejected the argument that deterrence and punishment are meaningless concepts to a child as young as 10 and stated that the imposition of a lengthy initial tariff on a child of this age to punish them would not amount to inhuman or degrading treatment within the meaning of the ECHR. A year later, Lord Woolf applied the welfare principle in re-fixing the minimum terms for Jon Venables and Robert Thompson in *Re Thompson (Tariff Recommendation)* [2001], having regard to the fact that a tariff of 8 years would prevent the two young men from being transferred to the young adult estate and being exposed to the 'corrosive atmosphere' of a YOI. He reduced the minimum term accordingly, such that Thompson and Venables were released on licence at the age of 18.

Section 91 PCC(S)A 2000

Section 91 PCC(S)A 2000 provides for longer terms of detention, greater than the usual maximum DTO available for children and young people. Section 91 sentences can only be imposed where a young person is convicted and sentenced in the Crown Court either:

- where the Youth Court declines jurisdiction on grounds that s. 91 sentencing powers ought to be available; or
- where a youth is jointly charged with an adult in relation to an offence to which s. 91 applies and the defendants are tried together in the Crown Court.

In effect such orders are available:

- where a young person aged 10–17 is convicted on indictment of either an offence punishable in the case of an adult with imprisonment of 14 years or more, or indecent assault on a man or a woman (the maximum sentence for both these offences, in the case of an adult, is 10 years);
- additionally, in the case of a young person aged 14–17 years convicted on indictment of causing death by dangerous driving, or causing death by careless driving while under the influence of drink or drugs (the maximum sentence for both these offences, in the case of an adult, is 10 years).

Where the above conditions are met, the court may make an order for long-term detention if it is of the opinion that 'no other method in which the case may legally be dealt with is suitable'.

In addition, s. 91 sentences are available for various sexual offences (even where the maximum sentence is less than 14 years or more) and certain offences relating to firearms. The length of sentence can be up to the adult maximum for the same offence, which for certain offences may be life. Once released, the young person is given a notice of supervision and is supervised by the YOT for a period of 3 months; conditions such as tagging can be applied during this period of supervision (ss 256B and 256C CJA 2003 as inserted by LASPO 2012).

The range of offences for which s. 91 sentences are available is perhaps surprising. The common understanding of 'grave' or serious offending is somewhat narrower than the legal concept of a grave crime (NACRO, 2002). Indeed, in principle at least, an offence of handling stolen goods committed by a 10-year-old child could fall within the remit of s. 91 (although in practice the Youth Court would invariably maintain jurisdiction). It is perhaps more obvious at the upper end of the scale of seriousness that certain offences might warrant longer sentences (for example, serious sexual or physical assaults, or armed robbery), but for offences such as residential burglary – particularly an opportunistic burglary resulting in a relatively small loss to the victim – the situation may be less clear (NACRO, 2002). Robbery also covers a broad range of behaviours: robbery is essentially defined as theft with violence or the threat of violence, but this could range from an incident of bullying including the theft of items of small value through to robbery from vulnerable victims using serious violence. Sentencing guidance and legislation, together with the YOT's recommendation in the PSR, aim to give consideration to the particular details of the case, such that mitigating circumstances can result in community sentences (such as a YRO with multiple requirements) being passed instead.

There is widespread debate about why certain offenders are prosecuted more harshly than others and why particular cases attract more public and political attention than others (a pertinent example being the killing of James Bulger in 1993; see key case analysis). There have been a number of other such extraordinary, emotive crimes, both in the UK and abroad, which have not had the intense and prolonged media reaction or influenced legislative changes in the way that this case has.

Dangerous offenders

The CJA 2003 introduced the concept of a 'dangerous offender'. The provisions introduced indeterminate sentences of imprisonment for public protection (IPP) and extended sentences for public protection (EPP) of imprisonment for dangerous sexual or violent offenders. These provisions came into effect on 4 April 2005 but, following widespread criticism (see, for example, Strickland, 2013), were abolished by the implementation of LASPO 2012 and replaced by the extended determinate sentence (EDS). However, in January 2014 there were 26 children and young people still serving IPP sentences, two serving EPP sentences (MoJ, 2014), and others remain on licence from s. 226 and s. 228 sentences, so the orders warrant mentioning here.

Section 226 CJA 2003: indeterminate sentences for public protection

If a child was convicted of a specified serious offence, and the court believed there was a significant risk to members of the public of serious harm as a result of further offences, the court could impose an IPP. Children were sentenced to a minimum tariff, after which they could apply to the Parole Board for release. This means that the child could be kept in prison after the end of the minimum tariff of imprisonment if they were still considered to be a risk to the public.

Section 228 CJA 2003: extended sentences for public protection

If a child was convicted of a certain violent or sexual offence, and the court considered there was a significant risk to members of the public of further offences, the court could impose an EPP. This means that the child would be subject to an extended period on licence, after release from custody.

Extended determinate sentences

Following its own review of IPPs, the Coalition government abolished IPPs and extended sentence provisions in the CJA 2003. LASPO 2012 introduced a new extended sentence for certain violent or sexual offences for those aged under 18 (s. 226B CJA 2003 as inserted by s. 124 LASPO 2012). The EDS consists of a custodial term, which should reflect the seriousness of the offending, followed by an extended licence period that is determined by the court on the basis of what the court considers 'necessary for the purpose of protecting members of the public from serious harm'. The extended licence period is limited to up to 5 years for a violent offence and 8 years for a sexual offence, and the sum of the custodial term and the extended licence must not exceed the maximum penalty for the offence. This means that a young person under the age of 18 may be sentenced under s. 124 if:

- he or she has been convicted of an offence listed in Schedule 15 CJA 2003 – this includes manslaughter, kidnapping and various sexual offences;
- the court believes that there is a significant risk to the public of serious harm by the offender of further offences specified in Schedule 15;
- the court does not consider a life sentence to be appropriate; but
- the current offence does warrant a custodial term of at least 4 years.

Young people aged under 18 sentenced to custody under any of the above orders will be placed within the juvenile secure estate, which is managed by the YJB.

The juvenile secure estate

There are three types of custodial institution for children and young people.

- Local authority secure children's homes (LASCHs) – at the time of writing there are 10 LASCHs, offering approximately 300 places for children aged 10–16 (Cavadino et al., 2013). These are small units and have the highest staff-to-child ratio in the children's secure estate, being between one member of staff to two children and six staff to eight children.
- STCs – the four STCs are run by private companies, offer approximately 300 places for boys and girls aged 12–17, and have a staff ratio of between two staff to five children and three staff to eight children. There is a mother and baby unit at Rainsbrook STC with space for three girls.
- YOIs – these hold boys aged 15–17. Most YOIs are run by HM Prison Service, with one (Parc) being privately run. YOIs have the lowest staff-to-child ratio in the juvenile secure estate, from just three to six staff for between 40 and 60 children on each wing.

Placement decisions

The initial decision as to where a child or young person is placed is taken by the YJB's placement team, taking into account:

- basic information (legal status, age, gender, location, court outcome);
- specific risk factors as identified by the relevant YOT;
- risk of harm;
- risk posed to others;
- previous history within the secure estate;
- specific needs, for example, the requirement for a specific programme of intervention, health education or welfare needs;
- the availability of places and competing demand for places;
- co-defendant/gang-related issues;
- YOT placement recommendation and presentation at court;
- discussions with prospective secure estate establishments to take into account the current mix of young people in those establishments.

The YJB aims to place children and young people as close to home as possible, but the target of being placed within 50 miles of home has been abandoned due to the decommissioning of places within the juvenile secure estate. For those serving longer-term sentences (s. 90/s. 91), decisions are taken in concert between the YJB and the casework section of the Prison Service. There are currently three long-term sentence units within YOIs which specifically cater for 15 to 17-year-olds who are serving indeterminate and long-term sentences, although the majority of young people serving long-term sentences are still held within mainstream YOIs (Howard League, 2010). Typically, young people will be transferred from LASCHs/STCs at the age of 15, although this has been subject to appeal, albeit unsuccessfully (*R (on the Application of ML) v Youth Justice Board* [2013]).

| *On-the-spot question* | What are the consequences of placing children and young people in institutions away from their homes? |

Characteristics of children in custody

Approximately 6 per cent of young people in custody are girls, and 96 per cent of those held in the secure estate in 2011/2012 were aged 15 to 17 (MoJ, 2013a). The discrimination apparent in other areas of the youth justice system culminates in the custodial estate: in 2011/2012 62 per cent of the young people held in custody were white, with 16 per cent being from a black ethnic background; 30 per cent of the black young people were held on remand, compared with 21 per cent of the white young people and 27 per cent of those who were Asian (MoJ, 2013a). The over-representation of black and minority ethnic (BME) young people is compounded by the disproportionate numbers of BME males with mental health and learning disabilities (Fox and Arnull, 2013; see also House of Commons Home Affairs Committee, 2007; and Chapter 1).

| *On-the-spot questions* | 1 What are the difficulties in meeting the needs of girls in custody?
2 What is the impact of racial discrimination in custody? |

Research has repeatedly highlighted the particularly disadvantaged and disrupted backgrounds of children serving custodial sentences, including high levels of abuse, witnessing or being subject to domestic violence, previous experience of homelessness, being looked after and/or being on the child protection register (Prison Reform Trust, 2011). Children in the juvenile secure estate are three times more likely to have a mental health problem than other young people (Hagell, 2002; Arnull et al., 2005), with eight out of ten meeting the criteria for more than one formal mental health diagnosis (Lader et al., 2000). Many children and young people in custody report hazardous levels of alcohol consumption and substance misuse prior to sentencing (Gould and Payne, 2004). Over half have been excluded from school, over a quarter have the literacy ability of an average 7-year-old and about a fifth have some form of learning disability (Bryan et al., 2007). It is clear that these children need particular support whilst in custody, much of which is provided by staff, including social workers, working within the secure estate. However, there is a significant role for social workers within the responsible YOT in terms of the duty of care held by the local authority for looked after children, under the Children Act 1989, and with regard to the resettlement of children and young people released from custody on licence (discussed below).

Concerns and breaches of rights within custody

Despite the positive work done by professionals within the youth justice system, questions remain as to whether custodial institutions are the most appropriate places for addressing the needs of some of these children (see, for example, Fox and Arnull, 2013). The UNCRC includes a requirement to separate children from adults in detention and recognizes that the right to education, health care, family life and protection from harm all still apply to children in detention. It is in this context that many serious breaches of children's rights occur.

Despite legislation stating that the imprisonment of children should only be considered as a last resort (discussed above), not all children in custody have committed serious or violent offences. Many children are given custodial sentences for non-violent crimes; for example, 16 per cent of the custodial population in 2011/2012 received custodial sentences for breach offences (MoJ, 2013a). A greater proportion of girls and younger children are in custody for breach than older boys, despite the fact that they are less likely to commit breach offences (Johns, 2011), suggesting discrimination against girls and younger children.

Furthermore, the welfare of the child can be overlooked, particularly within YOIs, due to the pressures of holding relatively large numbers of very troubled children together. Commentators have questioned the 'child-centredness' of juvenile custodial estate (Fox and Arnull, 2013), with Goldson and Coles (2005) describing the conditions within some secure establishments as 'institutional child abuse'. Whilst significant progress has been made in many areas, there are still worrying problems within youth secure estate. For example, between 1990 and 2012 32 children aged under 18 died whilst in custody, 31 of whom committed suicide; boys in prison are 18 times more likely to commit suicide than those of the same age in the community (Inquest, 2013). Official statistics reveal unacceptable rates of violence against children and young people in custody, including verbal, emotional, physical and sexual abuse (Drakeford and Butler, 2007; HM Chief Inspector of Prisons, 2013).

Contact with friends and family is limited, particularly as many young people are placed in institutions some considerable distance from their homes (MoJ, 2013a). Their education may be disrupted as the educational provision in custodial institutions is limited. While YOIs have a target of delivering 15 hours' education a week, on average they are only delivering 12 hours and an average of 9 per cent of young people in custody are not in work, education, training or offending behaviour programmes (Howard League, 2014). There is currently an apparent lack of commitment in enforcing legislation that ensures that local authorities take responsibility for the provision of education for children held in custody (Fox and Arnull, 2013). In an attempt to put 'education at the heart of custody', the Coalition government has legislated for a private 'secure college' to be built for 320–350 children and young people by 2017 (Criminal Justice and Courts Bill 2014). This proposal has received considerable criticism because, for example, it does not set out the structure, standards or programmes of the secure college nor creates a statutory right to education for children in custody, as recommended by the UN Committee on the Rights of the Child (2008). International standards also require that education be provided to young offenders outside detention facilities wherever possible, but the proposed secure college will provide education within secure facilities, further separating young people from the community and their peers, making reintegration more difficult (Anderson, 2013).

Behaviour management and restraint

The YJB has issued new guidance on behaviour management and restraint (Justice, 2013) after the restraint-related death of Gareth Myatt in 2004 (Inquest, 2012) and in response to increasing levels of restrictive physical interventions (RPIs) in the juvenile secure estate (MoJ, 2013a). However, there were almost 6500 incidents of physical restraint in 2012/2013, with an increase in RPIs per 100 young people of 45 per cent since 2009/2010 (MoJ, 2014). While guidance states that RPIs should only be used as a last resort to prevent harm to the young person or others, in 2012/2013 RPI was used an average of 538 times per month, involving an average of 366 young people. In 2.6 per cent of cases, the RPI resulted in a physical injury to the young person (MoJ, 2014). Girls are at a higher risk of being restrained, as are children aged 10 to 14 (MoJ, 2013a). The Criminal Justice and Courts Bill 2014 included a proposal to allow the use of force against children in custody to enforce 'good order and discipline', a practice which courts have previously deemed to be in breach of Article 3 ECHR.

On-the-spot question	How could the use of RPIs be minimized in custodial institutions?

Determining release dates

Determining the date at which a young person is released from custody is complex and varies according to the type/length of sentence; any period spent in custody on remand is deducted from the sentence and there are provisions for early release from fixed sentences, as there are for adults. Only a brief overview is given here (see further reading, below, for more detail).

- **Automatic release** – all children and young people serving fixed-length sentences (DTOs, s. 91 sentences and s. 228 sentences imposed after 14 July 2008) will have an automatic release date calculated for their sentence. They can only be detained past this date if additional days have been lawfully added by an independent adjudicator (s. 91 or s. 228 sentences) or court (DTO).
- **Early release** – children and young people serving DTOs of between 8 and 24 months and those serving s. 91 sentences of more than 3

months but less than 4 years (provided the offence is not an 'excluded' offence) are eligible for early release under an electronic tag under the Home Detention Curfew Scheme. There is a presumption of early release for the majority of children serving DTOs; suitable accommodation and support needs to be established in advance of the decision being made. If a child's application for early release is impossible because of a lack of resettlement plans, the interference with that child's right to liberty under Article 5 ECHR is considered especially serious in light of the duty under Article 37 UNCRC to make sure that children are detained for the shortest appropriate period of time (Howard League, 2013). Those serving DTOs of 8 to 16 months can be released up to a month before or after the halfway point; those serving sentences of 18 to 24 months can be released up to 1 or 2 months before or after the halfway point (s. 33 Offender Management Act 2007). The power to authorize an early release lies with the Secretary of State and acknowledges that young people may make very good progress in custody, as measured against their agreed sentence plan. In late release cases, where poor progress has been made by the young person, the Secretary of State must make an application to the Youth Court for an increased period of detention. Those with sentences of 4 years or more are presumed unsuitable for Home Detention Curfew and certain groups of offences are excluded from the scheme altogether. For example, under LASPO 2012, children and young people who have been convicted of a serious sexual or violent offence must serve at least two-thirds of their sentence before being eligible for release.

- **Release from indeterminate sentences** – children and young people serving indeterminate sentences (s. 90 and s. 91 PCC(S)A 2000; s. 226 CJA 2003) can only be released on the direction of the Parole Board (see below).

Licence and supervision

Once released from detention, all children and young people will be subject to a set of conditions; breach of these conditions can lead to an automatic recall to custody. Children serving DTOs are given a notice of supervision (s. 103 PCC(S)A 2000); those serving all other custodial sentences are released on licence and can be automatically recalled to prison by the Secretary of State for Justice if they breach the conditions of the licence. Depending on the nature of the breach, they will either be released again automatically after 28 days or at the discretion of the Parole Board.

Children serving s. 90 and s. 91 sentences will be released on a 'life licence': for s. 226 sentences, the licence will be at least 10 years and can only be cancelled by the Parole Board; for s. 228 sentences, the licence is for a set term and there is an automatic end date.

There are standard licence conditions including contact with the supervising officer, residing at an approved address, work and travel restrictions, and an expectation to 'be well behaved'. Additional conditions may include contact requirements, prohibited activities, programme requirements, supervision or drug testing. Supervision requirements and licence conditions are governed by Article 8 ECHR (the right to respect for private and family life); they are not designed to be punitive but are for the purposes of risk management and public protection (*R (on the Application of Carman) v Secretary of State for the Home Department* [2004], in Howard League, 2012). The conditions must be both necessary to protect the public and proportionate, balancing the right to private and family life with the need for public protection.

Parole

Children who are subject to indeterminate sentences must be assessed by the Parole Board for England and Wales in order to be released. The Parole Board's focus is on the potential risk to the public – if a young person is still considered to present a risk, they will not be released, otherwise they will be released on licence. The number of prisoners released by the Parole Board in recent years demonstrates that it has become increasingly risk averse. Consequently, there is a very small chance of release at the first review for all prisoners, including children (Howard League, 2010). There are a number of particular concerns for children and young people eligible for consideration by the Parole Board. For example, the focus of interventions in the juvenile secure estate is often education, rather than addressing offending behaviour – the former is not related to risk, and so it is difficult for Parole Board members to make a judgement on risk; and access to accredited offending behaviour programmes for children in the secure estate is extremely limited (Howard League, 2010). All secure units for children and young people have the same level of security so, although they may have some day visits, they are not tested in open conditions in the way that adults moving from high-security through to open prisons are, which may make the Parole Board's decision harder to make. Children and young people are often released to the same area they came from, with the same negative influences and disadvantages, whereas adults can be released to approved locations where the temptation to reoffend is perhaps not so great (Howard League, 2010). A lack of knowledge about the parole process for children and inadequate provision can cause significant delays, misunderstandings and gaps in the process (Howard League, 2010). Although parole decisions affect only a very small number of children and young people each year, their needs and rights should not be overlooked in policy or practice (see further reading, below).

Resettlement

Planning for release and resettlement work should begin shortly after admission to custody, with a planning meeting being held between the YOT, young person, parents and the custodial establishment (Johns, 2011). The local authority has a duty under the Children Act 1989 to accommodate a child or young person aged under 16 if they cannot return home on release; with parental consent they can become looked after, otherwise children's services may have to start care proceedings. If the young person is aged 16 or over, and does not consent to being looked after, they could be housed under the Housing Act 1996; it is unusual for care proceedings to be taken (Howard League, 2012).

The YJB has established a number of local and national resettlement consortia and initiatives, with the aim of developing and providing a more comprehensive service for children and young people leaving custody. Young people released from custody may face difficulties in finding appropriate accommodation and employment or in accessing financial support and benefits; they may require ongoing mental health or substance abuse treatment; and they may lack emotional support (Howard League, 2012). Children and young people in consortia areas receive extra support with training, accommodation and employment to help them avoid reoffending. However, funding for these initiatives – such as the use of 'resettlement brokers' in the Heron Unit at Feltham YOI – has been cut, seemingly at odds with the government's wider efforts to give greater priority to rehabilitation.

> ◣ **PRACTICE FOCUS**
>
> Michael, aged 16, is serving an 18-month DTO in a YOI. He was convicted of causing arson being reckless as to whether the life of another would be thereby endangered, having accidently set fire to a garden shed where he was sleeping after being thrown out of his home by his parents. Michael has a volatile relationship with his parents and has been looked after in a number of temporary respite foster placements during his childhood. He has a history of offending behaviour, largely acquisitive offences relating to being homeless but also convictions for possession of cannabis and public order offences.
>
> • What is the role of the social worker while Michael is in custody?
> • What are the implications for Michael of having been a looked after child?
> • What plans need to put in place for Michael's release?

Criminal records

LASPO 2012 introduced changes to the Rehabilitation of Offenders Act 1974, with regard to when convictions are considered 'spent', which were then enacted in the Offender Rehabilitation Act 2014. In recognition of the developing nature of children and young people and the stigmatizing impact of criminal records on rehabilitation, convictions for children generally become 'spent' in half the time applicable for adults, although custodial sentences of 4 or more years are never spent. Youth cautions, absolute discharges and reparation orders are spent immediately and do not need to be declared (although they will be recorded on the Police National Computer); referral orders are considered spent at the end of the period of the order; YCCs are spent after 3 months; and fines after 6 months. Community sentences, including YROs, are spent 6 months from the end date of the sentence; custodial sentences of under 6 months are spent after 18 months, those of 6 to 30 months are spent after 2 years, and those of 2.5 to 4 years are spent after 3.5 years. Reducing the length of time before an order is spent is a beneficial development which may help young people re-enter education or find training or employment and thus have a positive impact on recidivism, but it is still of concern that children and young people with criminal records may face ongoing discrimination.

Conclusions

Theory and practice both suggest custody itself can be criminogenic. Theories of differential association (Sutherland, 1947) argue that young people sentenced to custody will meet other, more experienced young offenders and potentially learn from them, learning different techniques, ways of avoiding being caught and how to 'work the system', as well as developing anti-authority attitudes (Howard League, 1998). Labelling theory (Becker, 1963) demonstrates how being sentenced to custody can be stigmatizing and often has negative consequences for young people once they have been released, in terms of finding employment and accommodation, particularly as they will have an 'active' criminal record for a minimum of 18 months post-release. As a result, almost three-quarters (73 per cent) of young people released from custody reoffend within a year of their release, compared with 68 per cent of those who receive a YRO and 45 per cent of those who received other community sentences (MoJ, 2013a).

It is thus essential to continue the reduction in the youth justice population and, for those who remain within the juvenile secure estate, to improve the conditions therein, both to ensure that their rights are not breached and to maximize rehabilitation and minimize recidivism. The discrimination apparent against girls and some minority ethnic groups, both at the point of sentencing and during the custodial period itself, needs to be addressed, and the particular needs of those children serving long-term sentences warrant detailed consideration. Any period of custody risks breaching children and young people's rights and a custodial sentence, be it short or long-term, can only be justified if it does offer a valid opportunity for rehabilitation and positive reintegration after release, and if the welfare of the child is prioritized. The final chapter of this book reflects on the tensions inherent within the youth justice system and upon the importance of upholding children's rights.

Further reading

Howard League for Penal Reform (2009) *Analysis of the Inspectorate of Prisons Reports on Young Offender Institutions Holding Children in Custody* gives an overview of HM Inspectorate of Prisons' reports into the conditions experienced by children and young people within the juvenile secure estate.

Howard League for Penal Reform (2012) *Resettlement: The Legal Rights of Children and Young People in the Criminal Justice System in Need of Accommodation and Support* provides a detailed overview of the resettlement process, including release, licence periods and the legal rights to accommodation under the Children Act 1989 and the Housing Act 1996.

MoJ/NOMS (2012) *The Transition Process: Guidance on Transfers from Under 18 Young Offender Institutions to Young Adult Young Offender Institutions –* this protocol includes advice for practitioners working in custody in both under-18 and young adult YOIs on preparing young people for transfer to the adult secure estate, the processes that should be followed before, during and after transfer, effective information-sharing and relationship-building and ensuring that the young person, their family and/or carers are fully involved throughout the process.

NACRO, Beyond Youth Custody programme – a 5-year national programme that aims to establish an evidence base of effective practice with young people and young adults leaving custody and to engage with practitioners and policymakers to develop sustainable models of resettlement that can be delivered and adopted on a national scale www.beyondyouthcustody.net/.

Parole Board guidance – gives details of the parole process and provides updates on legislative changes to the process that affect children and young people www.justice.gov.uk/offenders/parole-board.

6
CONCLUSIONS

AT A GLANCE THIS CHAPTER COVERS:

- recent progress
- developments in the adult justice system
- developments in the Family Court
- tensions for practitioners working within youth justice
- upholding children's rights

Recent progress

Significant progress has been made in meeting the primary aim of the youth justice system – to prevent offending – with fewer first-time entrants to the system, resulting in fewer community and custodial sentences being passed. The success of YOTs in developing holistic, multi-agency working with young people who offend has partly resulted from policy changes, with a heightened focus on diversion, early intervention and prevention, and increased scope for professional discretion, and partly from demands for financial savings and economic constraints. The progress made also reflects a greater recognition of the potential vulnerability of children and young people involved in offending behaviour and the need to align youth justice legislation with the ECHR, the UNCRC and the Human Rights Act 1998. However, caution is still needed – youth justice's position as a key 'political football' suggests that the relentless pace of change is likely to continue. Recent history has shown that numerous initiatives have been introduced without being allowed to bed in or become fully operational before they are superseded by the next big idea (Hucklesby and Wahidin, 2013), and there is no reason to believe that this will change. For the last half-century, political parties have sought to sell their criminal justice policies to the electorate; there is an important populist element in the way policy is formed, with the shared assumption that being tough on crime and claiming to promote the interests of victims rather than defendants will bring electoral success (Ashworth and Redmayne, 2010). Although defeated in its attempts, the Coalition's desire to widen the scope of civil injunctions against 'nuisance and annoyance' suggests that it believes that tough early intervention is needed, with zero tolerance for the transgressions made by children and young people.

However, despite a generally repressive penal climate, the increased focus on diversion (Chapters 1 and 2) is to be (cautiously) lauded, although monitoring of its use is essential to ensure that it does not increase the likelihood that young people will be stigmatized, labelled, drawn into the system and 'up-tariffed' (Cavadino et al., 2013). Diversion has benefits over formal prosecution – diversionary interventions can be an efficient way of closing the 'justice gap' by resolving more offences; diversion is far less expensive and time-consuming than formal prosecutions; evidence suggests diversions are more effective (or at least, no less effective) than formal interventions in preventing recidivism and have far fewer negative consequences for children and young people. However, it is possible that considerations of cost and sanction detection rates weigh more heavily with policy-makers than does an ideological approach of maximum diversion and minimum intervention that is sensitive to the needs of young offenders (Ashworth and Redmayne, 2010; McAra and McVie, 2010), meaning that the commitment to diversionary activities may waver in the future. As Souhami (2013:236) states: 'Reforms based on financial imperatives are of course unstable and youth justice remains a volatile political field.'

Developments in the adult justice system

While the youth justice system is in some ways a discrete entity, it is influenced by developments in the adult system. These developments may have a direct impact (for example, the implementation of adult-centric procedures like MAPPA and parole within the youth justice system) and it is imperative that children's needs and rights are considered when legislative or practice changes are mooted within the adult justice system that may impact upon children. In a personal reflection, Bache (2013), the chair of the Youth Courts Committee of the Magistrates' Association, made a pertinent comment that:

> … youth justice is frequently forgotten when new legislation or new initiatives are introduced. This is not an active intention but a passive result of the relative invisibility of youth justice. 'Out of sight is out of mind'. If politicians and others in positions of influence are not reminded that children and young people below the age of eighteen are not adults, they will conveniently dismiss them from their thoughts.
>
> *Bache, 2013:12*

Other changes may impact on young people as they move from the youth justice system into the adult system. For instance, under the Offender Rehabilitation Act 2014 the government is introducing mandatory one-year community supervision for first-time offenders who are in custody for less than 12 months. The legislation includes all offenders aged over 18 when they are released, even if they were under 18 when sentenced. The government hopes that increasing the length of time young offenders who turn 18 during their sentence are supervised in the community will cut reoffending but there are concerns that young people will be returned to custody for breaching the conditions of their supervision, as happened with the implementation of ASBOs.

The government's recent proposals to end specialist custodial institutions for 18 to 21-year-olds have also caused some disquiet. If implemented, this would have a direct impact on young adults, who would be placed within adult institutions, but also on children being transferred from the juvenile secure estate to the adult estate (MoJ, 2013c). The transition from youth to young adult custody is already problematic; for example, despite guidance to practitioners on managing the transition process, young people transferring to the young adult system often 'fall through the cracks' in services, including mental health provision (Centre for Mental Health, 2014). A decision on these proposals has been delayed until after the publication of a review of self-inflicted deaths of 18 to 24-year-olds in custody (expected in spring 2015), but if it they are approved, they will have significant implications for the transition process from juvenile to adult estate.

Developments in the Family Court

Similarly, the youth justice system may be directly and indirectly influenced by developments within the Family Court (renamed by the Crime and Courts Act 2013) and within child welfare legislation. For instance, there have been calls for greater integration between child welfare proceedings and youth justice hearings to allow, in exceptional circumstances of significant welfare need, for a child prosecuted in the Youth Court to be referred to the Family Court. The Crime and Courts Bill Committee discussed adding a new clause to the Bill to this effect, although this was not included in the final Crime and Courts Act 2013. However, other jurisdictions have demonstrated the benefits of a more integrated response; for example, in 2010 the New York Department of Juvenile Justice was subsumed within the Administration for Children's Services, recognizing that, in order to break the cycle of delinquency, juvenile misbehaviour should be seen, first and foremost, as a child welfare issue (Bates and Swan, 2014). While the current Coalition government has confirmed that it considers the Youth Court to be best equipped to determine guilt and, where necessary, the appropriate sentence, future governments may take a different stance and promote an integrated response to children's offending behaviour.

Tensions for practitioners working within youth justice

Despite New Labour's reforms of the youth justice system, it remains incoherent and has no clear orientation; the overarching aim of 'preventing offending' is so broad that it can be used to justify almost any youth justice practice (Souhami, 2013). Rather than clarifying the approach that should be taken, the reforms perpetuated the competing legal frameworks of welfare and justice that can lead to tensions for social workers and other practitioners working within the system. Coupled with entrenched, value-laden views of children and young people, these complex and potentially incompatible approaches to working with children and young people who offend can lead to ethical dilemmas for practitioners and can cause them to question their professional value-base. Practitioners may also be faced with the challenges presented by multi-agency and inter-agency working; by its nature, there are a range of different professionals within a YOT and practitioners also need to work with the police, court staff and legal professionals and, where applicable, custodial staff – organizations where there may be strong occupational cultures and expectations (Ashworth and Redmayne, 2010). There is a need for practitioners to recognize and understand these different professional perspectives but it can be difficult to retain a child-focused welfare approach and social work identity that promotes the recognition of diversity, equality and non-oppressive practice alongside colleagues who may take a neo-correctionalist or justice approach (Pickford and Dugmore, 2012).

Discretion is an important principle within the youth justice system, allowing individual circumstances to be considered, but the use of discretion can lead to unfair practices and differential treatment; wherever there is discretion, and even where there are rules, there may be choices between following ethical principles and following other policies or preferences. Although, in terms of legislation, the welfare of the child is paramount, this can conflict with the principles of justice, victims' rights and public safety; different professionals within the youth justice system may ideologically favour the latter elements over the welfare of a child who has caused harm to others.

Furthermore, the professional role is not static and during the course of any intervention a practitioner may have to adapt to the particular requirements applicable at different stages of the youth justice system. For example, they may have to conduct an assessment of a young person and act as an advocate for them but also as an advisor and enforcer to the courts (Fox and Arnull, 2013). To conduct a meaningful assessment or recommend an appropriate intervention, a practitioner needs to build a rapport with a young person and gain their trust; however, as an enforcer, they may need to confront particular attitudes and behaviour demonstrated by the young person, which may threaten the relationship between the practitioner and young person. As an advocate, a practitioner may need to advise on sentencing – ensuring that the sentence passed is commensurate with the offence and facilitates access to appropriate services – promote anti-oppressive and anti-discriminatory practice, and be prepared to challenge decisions made about the young person. Conversely, practitioners must also be prepared to report a young person for possible breaches of orders, even if this may lead to an apparently negative outcome (such as a return to custody) for the young person.

The impact of the increasing involvement of voluntary and community sector organizations on the ethos and practices of the youth justice system will soon become apparent. Similarly, the increasing privatization of parts of the system and the introduction of payment-by-results could lead to significant changes in the way that youth justice services are commissioned and delivered, although opposition to both privatization and payment-by-results on ethical, legal and ideological grounds is likely to continue (Hucklesby and Wahidin, 2013). The increasing localism agenda and decrease in ring-fencing of funding has already resulted in a lack of consistency in police and YOT services across different local authorities (CRAE, 2013), and the further fracturing of service delivery through the use of a wider range of private and third-sector organizations could contribute to discrepancies and differential treatment across the youth justice system. While it is important to develop new interventions and strategies that are relevant to the needs of local communities, variations in practice should be monitored and only sanctioned if there is clear justification for differences to ensure that principles of anti-discrimination, equality and anti-oppression are upheld.

Upholding children's rights

There is a need for those working within youth justice to promote the rights of children and young people involved in offending behaviour, particularly in light of the potentially hostile public attitudes towards them, and youth justice practitioners should defend children's human rights 'with vigour' (NACRO, 2008). Respect for rights should be seen as a concomitant aim of the justice process, not merely a side constraint (Ashworth and Redmayne, 2010). Despite some positive progress, such as extending the right to appropriate adults to 17-year-olds, a range of breaches of the UNCRC and ECHR continue, not least the comparatively very low MACR, the restricted right to silence, changes to the availability of legal aid, the continued use of custody, both for pre-trial detention and as punishment, and the limitations to the right to anonymity in both civil and criminal proceedings.

Criminal justice policy statements pay limited attention to rights, with children's rights being either not considered or too lightly dismissed:

> In this country, the spirit underlying the United Nations Convention on the Rights of the Child does not pervade Government pronouncements on youth justice, and the desire for vote-winning headlines seems to be thought more important. (Ashworth and Redmayne, 2010:425)

There are particular concerns for younger children; recent policy and legislative changes have increasingly treated 10 to 14-year-olds as fully competent, aware of the significance and repercussions of their actions and mature enough to accept responsibility for them, resulting in a trend towards increasingly intrusive interventions for younger children. These policy changes appear to have been politically motivated rather than based on any real change in the nature of childhood or the competence of children and practitioners need to be prepared to challenge such disregard of children's rights and welfare needs.

All children and young people may be subject to the increasingly risk-averse atmosphere that appears dominant in many areas of practice, which may lead to defensive decision-making and a culture of blame. Within youth justice, this has influenced models of community protection that are characterized by the use of restriction, surveillance, monitoring and control, and compulsory treatment, which may be oppressive (Gelsthorpe, 2013). The increasing use of diversionary measures is a two-edged sword; whilst it avoids the potentially negative implications of full prosecution, it can lead to repressive welfarism and practice based on notions of risk that do not need evidence of guilt or even for an offence to have occurred (Souhami, 2013). Furthermore, the decision to prosecute a young person or to divert them from the formal justice system and/or impose an out-of-court disposal raises questions of principle about the proper role of courts and the amount and type of discretion law enforcement agencies should be allowed to wield (Ashworth and Redmayne, 2010).

Alongside individual practitioners working to uphold children's rights within the youth justice system, there are a range of other bodies that can be called upon to address potential breaches of rights or harmful practice. For example, the Independent Police Complaints Commission oversees the police complaints system and can be utilized to question the behaviour of police in stop and search procedures, arrests or detention within a police station. The Criminal Cases Review Commission can review cases that have exhausted the appeals process and refer them back to the Court of Appeal if appropriate, whilst the Prisons and Probation Ombudsman and Independent Monitoring Boards can respond to complaints and concerns raised by children in custody. Furthermore, children's rights and penal campaign organizations, such as the CRAE, the Howard League for Penal Reform and the Penal Reform Trust, continue to lobby the government for legislative change to uphold children's rights within the justice system.

Ultimately, unless youth justice is removed from the political arena, it will continue to be influenced by competing political motives, resulting in disjointed legislation and a system which may not always be in the best interests of the child. There is a need for long-term stability and continuity, which requires a cross-party consensus (Gelsthorpe, 2013) and the reconstruction of youth offending as an apolitical issue. Offending behaviour is in itself a social construct, the definitions of which vary across time and place, which demands a broader social response, taking into consideration wider social structures, legislation and policies. Any reform is likely to have only a modest impact if only part of the system is addressed, or if social structures and related policies remain little changed (Ashworth and Redmayne, 2010). A more holistic reform of responses to children involved in offending behaviour is needed in order to achieve significant, lasting improvements.

KEY SOURCES AND USEFUL WEBSITES

Journals

Journals such as *Youth Justice: An International Journal*, the *British Journal of Criminology* and the *Howard Journal of Criminal Justice* provide regular updates on developments in the youth/criminal justice system and legal commentaries, as well as more in-depth research-based articles.

Journals such as *Child and Adolescent Social Work Journal*, the *Journal of Youth and Adolescence*, *Child and Family Social Work*, *Childhood* and *Children and Society* also contain relevant research articles.

Further information about the youth justice system, including legislation, policy and practice developments, and campaigns can be found at the websites listed below.

Websites

Beyond Youth Justice
www.beyondyouthcustody.net

Centre for Social Justice
www.centreforsocialjustice.org.uk

Child and Maternal Health Intelligence Network: Youth Justice Hub
www.chimat.org.uk/youthjustice

Criminal Justice Alliance
www.criminaljusticealliance.org

Crown Prosecution Service
www.cps.gov.uk

Howard League for Penal Reform
www.howardleague.org

Gov.uk
www.gov.uk/browse/justice

Legislation
www.legislation.gov.uk

National Appropriate Adult Network
www.appropriateadult.org.uk

NACRO
www.nacro.org.uk

National Association for Youth Justice
www.thenayj.org.uk

Parole Board
www.gov.uk/government/organisations/parole-board

Prison Reform Trust
www.prisonreformtrust.org.uk

Standing Committee for Youth Justice
www.scyj.org.uk

The Advocates Gateway
www.theadvocatesgateway.org

UNICEF and the UNCRC
www.unicef.org/crc/

Youth Justice Board for England and Wales
www.justice.gov.uk/youth-justice

GLOSSARY

Appropriate adult
An independent adult appointed to provide a safeguard for a child aged under 18 who is arrested and/or detained by the police, introduced by PACE 1984.

ASSET/ASSETPlus
The national assessment framework for children and young people involved in the youth justice system (see also ONSET), developed by the YJB.

Criminogenic
Tending to produce crime or offending behaviour.

Detention and training order
The most commonly used determinate custodial sentence for children and young people.

Deviancy amplification
A cycle of increasing numbers of (media) reports on a category of antisocial behaviour or some other 'undesirable' event, leading to a 'moral panic', which then leads to more punitive responses.

Differential association
The theory that criminal behaviour is learnt through exposure to pro-criminal values and behaviours.

Doli incapax
The fourteenth-century principle that children under a certain age are incapable of criminal intent; until 1998 was applicable to children aged 10 to 14 but this was abolished in the Crime and Disorder Act 1998.

Indictable offences
Offences that must be tried at the Crown Court (including murder, manslaughter, rape, robbery and other 'grave' offences) (see also summary offences and triable-either-way offences).

Labelling
The process by which social reaction (stigmatization, stereotyping etc.) to an individual causes greater involvement in offending behaviour.

Managerialism
Performance-oriented approach to the delivery of public services, based on efficiency, key performance indicators and measurable targets.

Moral panic
An instance of heightened public anxiety or alarm in response to a problem regarded as threatening the moral standards of society. It may result in a disproportionate response being taken to the initial problem (see also deviancy amplification).

Net-widening
The process by which attempts to prevent crime draw more individuals into the youth justice system.

Notifiable offences
Those offences which require the police to record an incident as a crime and report the occurrence to the Home Office.

ONSET
The national assessment framework for young children identified as being 'at risk' of involvement in offending or anti-social behaviour (see also ASSET/ASSETPlus).

Positivism
Theoretical perspective that attempts to use 'scientific' methods to identify the key causes of crime – includes biological, sociological and psychological approaches.

Pre-sentence report
A report written by the YOT for the sentencing magistrates or judges detailing information about the offence, the child or young person's background, their offending history and responses to any previous interventions, and making a recommendation on the most appropriate sentence to help inform the sentencing decision.

Recidivism
Proven reoffending behaviour after a youth justice sentence or intervention. Recidivism rates for children and young people are often calculated for one year post-intervention.

Referral order
The primary sentence for children and young people convicted in court for the first time; requires the child or young person to attend a YOP and agree a contract of reparation and appropriate interventions to help prevent recidivism.

Risk, needs and responsivity
The principles of risk, needs and responsivity are used to inform the appropriate level of intervention within the scaled approach to sentencing.

Risk/protective factors
Factors that are highly correlated with the risk of offending/desistance from offending, including family background and family relationships, peer relationships, substance misuse, and neighbourhood and community factors – identified largely through positivist research (see also positivism) and used to inform the ASSETPlus/ONSET national assessment frameworks.

Scaled approach
An approach to sentencing based on progressive interventions of increasing intensiveness for each successive offence, underpinned by the risk, needs and responsivity framework.

Special measures
Measures introduced by the YJCE 1999 to assist vulnerable witnesses in court, e.g. giving evidence by video-link.

Standard of proof
The level to which a case must be proven in court. In criminal matters the standard of proof is 'beyond reasonable doubt', in civil matters it is on a 'balance of probabilities'.

Summary offences
Offences tried only by a Magistrates' Court, such as motoring offences, criminal damage, common assault (see also indictable offences and triable-either-way offences).

Triable-either-way offences
Offences which may be tried either at the Crown Court or at a Magistrates' Court, such as theft, burglary, driving under the influence (often amalgamated for statistical purposes with indictable offences).

Youth caution/youth conditional caution
Out-of-court disposals for minor offending or anti-social behaviour. They replaced the system of reprimands and final warnings and were introduced in LASPO 2012.

Youth Justice Board
Executive non-departmental public body that oversees the youth justice system in England and Wales, established by the CDA 1998.

Youth offending teams
Multi-agency teams, arranged by local authorities and overseen by the YJB, which engage in a wide variety of work with young offenders to reduce reoffending and recidivism. Established by the CDA 1998, they include representatives from the police, probation, education, health and social services.

Youth rehabilitation order
A generic community sentence for children and young people that can be tailored to an individual through the imposition of relevant 'requirements' from a list of 18 possible requirements, such as supervision, attendance centre, or IF.

Youth restorative disposal
An out-of-court disposal used by the police in conjunction with the YOT for minor offending or anti-social behaviour – based on the principles of restorative justice.

BIBLIOGRAPHY

Allen, C, I Crow and M Cavadino (2000) *Evaluation of the Youth Court Demonstration Project*, Home Office Research Study No 214 (London: Home Office)

Anderson, K (2013) 'Education for children in custody', *Children and Young People Now*, 30 April–13 May, 27

Arnull, E and S Eagle (2009) *Girls Offending: Patterns, Perceptions and Interventions* (London: Youth Justice Board)

Arnull, E, S Eagle, A Gammampila, K Miller and D Archer (2005) *A Retrospective Study of Persistent Young Offenders,* Final Report to Youth Justice Board (London: Youth Justice Board)

Ashworth, A and M Redmayne (2010) *The Criminal Process* 4th edn (Oxford: Oxford University Press)

Audit Commission (1996) *Misspent Youth* (Abingdon: Audit Commission Publications)

Bache, J (2013) 'Eternal vigilance: the price of youth justice' 69(5) *Magistrate* 12

Baker, K (2005) 'Assessment in youth justice: professional discretion and the use of Asset' 5(2) *Youth Justice* 106–22

Baker, K (2009) 'Sentencing young people' in M Blyth, R Newman and C Wright (eds), *Children and Young People in Custody* (Bristol: The Policy Press) 45–54

Baker, K, G Kelly and B Wilkinson B (2011) *Assessment in Youth Justice* (Bristol: Policy Press)

Ball, C (2014) *Focus on Social Work Law: Looked After Children* (Basingstoke: Palgrave Macmillan)

Bateman, T (2009) 'The rising tide of girl crime' 65(5) *Magistrate* 2–3

Bates, K A and R S Swan (2014) *Juvenile Delinquency in a Diverse Society* (London: Sage)

Becker, H (1963) *Outsiders: Studies in the Sociology of Deviance* (New York: Free Press)

Bell, C (2013) 'Detention of children: who's looking out for them?' 69(10) *Magistrate* 9

Bottoms, A E (2004) 'Empirical research relevant to sentencing frameworks' in A Bottoms, S Rex and G Robinson (eds), *Alternatives to Prison: Options for an Insecure Society* (Cullompton: Willan) 59–82

Bradley Report (2009) *Lord Bradley's Review of People with Mental Health Problems or Learning Disabilities in the Criminal Justice System* (London: Department of Health)

Brown, K J (2013) 'Replacing the ASBO with the injunction to prevention nuisance and annoyance: a plea for legislative scrutiny and amendment', Legislative Comment, 8 *Criminal Law Review* 623–39

Bryan, K, J Freer and C Furlong (2007) 'Language and communication difficulties in juvenile offenders' 42(5) *International Journal of Language and Communication Disorders* 505–20

Campbell, L and N Lynch (2012) 'Competing paradigms: the use of DNA powers in youth justice' 12(3) *Youth Justice* 3–18

Care Quality Commission (2014) *Monitoring the Mental Health Act in 2012/13*, presented to Parliament by the Secretary of State for Health pursuant to s. 120D(3) MHA 1983

Case, S (2007) 'Questioning the "evidence" of risk that underpins evidence-led youth justice interventions' 7(2) *Youth Justice* 91–105

Case, S and K Haines (2009) *Understanding Youth Offending: Risk Factor Research, Policy and Practice* (Cullompton: Willan)

Cavadino, M, J Dignan and G Mair (2013) *The Penal System: An Introduction* 5th edn (London: Sage)

Cemlyn, S, M Greenfields, S Burnett, Z Matthews and C Whitwell (2009) *Inequalities Experienced by Gypsy and Traveller Communities: A Review* (Manchester: Equality and Human Rights Commission)

Centre for Mental Health (2014) *Young Adults (18–24) in Transition: Mental Health and Criminal Justice,* The Bradley Commission Briefing (London: Centre for Mental Health)

Children's Legal Centre (undated) *At the Police Station: The Role of the 'Appropriate Adult'*, Legal Guide (Colchester: Children's Legal Centre)

Children's Rights Alliance for England (2013) *State of Children's Rights in England 2013* (London: Children's Rights Alliance for England) www.crae.org.uk/publications-resources/state-of-childrens-rights-in-england-2013

Children's Society (2000a) *National Remand Rescue Initiative: Work at HMP and YOI Doncaster, 1st January 1999 to 30th November 1999* (London: Children's Society)

Children's Society (2000b) *National Remand Rescue Initiative: Work at HM YOI and RC Feltham, 1st January 1999 to 30th November 1999* (London: Children's Society)

Children's Society, Criminal Justice Alliance, JUSTICE and Standing Committee for Youth Justice (2013) *Briefing and Suggested Amendments on Anti-social Behaviour, Crime and Policing Bill, House of Lords Report Stage* http://scyj.org.uk/wp-content/uploads/2013/12/Joint-HL-Report-Stage-Briefing-on-ASB.pdf

Cohen, S (1972) *Folk Devils and Moral Panics* (London: MacGibbon & Kee)

Coram Children's Legal Centre (2013) *The Implications for Access to Justice of the Government's Proposed Legal Aid Reforms: Coram Children's Legal Centre Evidence to the Joint Committee on Human Rights inquiry* www.childrens legalcentre.com/userfiles/JCHR_legal_aid_inquiry_evidence_Coram_ Childrens_Legal_Centre.pdf

Crawford, A and T Newburn (2002) 'Recent developments in restorative justice for young people in England and Wales: community participation and representation' 42(3) *British Journal of Criminology* 476–95

Crawford, A and T Newburn (2003) *Youth Offending and Restorative Justice: Implementing Reform in Youth Justice* (Cullompton: Willan)

Crofts, T (2009) 'Doli incapax: in defence of a defence' 252 *ChildRight* 19–21

Crown Prosecution Service (undated) *Legal Guidance: Youth Offenders* www.cps.gov.uk/legal/v_to_z/youth_offenders/

Crown Prosecution Service (2013) *The Director's Guidance on Youth Conditional Cautions: Guidance to Police Officers and Crown Prosecutors*, issued by the Director of Public Prosecutions under s. 37A of PACE 1984 2nd edn www.cps.gov.uk/publications/directors_guidance/youth_ conditional_cautions.html

Cunningham, H (2006) *The Invention of Childhood* (London: BBC Books)

Department for Children, Schools and Families (2003) *Every Child Matters*, CM 5860 (London: The Stationery Office)

Department for Children, Schools and Families (2007) *The Children's Plan: Building Brighter Futures*, Cm 7280 (London: The Stationery Office)

Department for Children, Schools and Families, Home Office, Youth Justice Board and Association of Chief Police Officers (2009) *Safer School Partnerships Guidance* (London: The Stationery Office)

Department for Education (2011) *The Core Purpose of Sure Start Children's Centres* (London: Department for Education) http://media.education. gov.uk/assets/files/pdf/s/sure%20start%20childrens%20centres%20core %20purpose.pdf

Department for Education (2013) *Working Together to Safeguard Children* (London: Department for Education) www.gov.uk/government/policies/ supporting-social-workers-to-provide-help-and-protection-to-children

Department of Health (2014) *Mental Health Crisis Care Concordat: Improving Outcomes for People Experiencing Mental Health Crisis* (London:

Department of Health and Home Office) www.gov.uk/government/ publications/mental-health-crisis-care-agreement

Department of Work and Pensions (2012) *Social Justice: Transforming Lives*, Cm 8314 (London: The Stationery Office)

Drakeford, M and I Butler (2007) 'Everyday tragedies: justice, scandal and young people in contemporary Britain' 46(3) *Howard Journal of Criminal Justice* 219–35

Drizin, S A and R A Leo (2004) 'The problem of false confessions in post-DNA world' 82 *North Carolina Law Review* 891–1007

Earle, R (2005) 'The referral order' in T Bateman and J Pitts (eds), *The RHP Companion to Youth Justice* (Lyme Regis: Russell House)

Ellison, G (2013) 'Policing: context and practice' in A Hucklesby and A Wahidin (eds), *Criminal Justice* 2nd edn (Oxford: Oxford University Press) 57–82

Equality and Human Rights Commission (2010) *Stop and Think: A Critical Review of the Use of Stop and Search Powers in England and Wales* (Manchester: Equality and Human Rights Commission)

Fair Play for Children (2011) *The Compatibility of Acceptable Behaviour Contracts with Article 6.1 of the European Convention on Human Rights* www.fairplayforchildren.org/index.php?page=Playaction_Guides&section =Publications

Farrington, D P and B C Welsh (2007*) Saving Children from a Life of Crime: Early Risk Factors and Effective Interventions* (Oxford: Oxford University Press)

Fionda, J (2005) *Devils or Angels: Youth, Policy and Crime* (Oxford: Hart)

Fisher, P A and P Chamberlain (2000) 'Multidimensional Treatment Foster Care: a program for intensive parenting, family support, and skill building' 8 *Journal of Emotional and Behavioral Disorders* 155–64

Fitzgerald, M (1993) *Ethnic Minorities and the Criminal Justice System*, The Royal Commission on Criminal Justice, Research Study No 20 (London: HMSO)

Flood-Page, C and A Mackie (1998) *Sentencing Practice: An Examination of Decisions in Magistrates' Courts and the Crown Court in the mid-1990s*, Home Office Research Study No 180 (London: Home Office) cited by M Cavadino, J Dignan and G Mair (2013) *The Penal System: An Introduction* 5th edn (London: Sage)

Fox, C and K Albertson (2011) 'Payment by results and social impact bonds in the criminal justice sector: new challenges for the concept of evidence-based policy?' 11(5) *Criminology and Criminal Justice* 395–413

Fox, D and E Arnull (2013) *Social Work in the Youth Justice System: A Multidisciplinary Perspective* (Maidenhead: Open University Press)

Fyson, R and J Yates (2011) 'Anti-social behaviour orders and young people with learning disabilities' 31(1) *Critical Social Policy* 102–25

Gelsthorpe, L (2013) 'Criminal justice: the policy landscape' in A Hucklesby and A Wahidin (eds), *Criminal Justice* 2nd edn (Oxford: Oxford University Press) 17–33

Goldson, B and D Coles (2005) *In the Care of the State: Child Deaths in Penal Custody in England and Wales* (London: Inquest)

Goldson, B and J Muncie (2006) 'Editors' Introduction' in B Goldson and J Muncie (eds), *Youth Crime and Justice: Critical Issues* (London: Sage) ix–xiv

Gould, J and H Payne (2004) 'Health needs of children in prison' 89(6) *Archives of Disease in Childhood* 500–1

Gudjonsson, G, J F Sigurdsson and I D Sigfusdottir (2009) 'False confessions among 15 and 16 year olds in compulsory education and the relationship with adverse life events' 20(6) *Journal of Forensic Psychiatry and Psychology* 950–96

Hagell, A (2002) *The Mental Health of Young Offenders: Bright Futures – Working with Vulnerable Young People* (London: Mental Health Foundation)

Halsey, K and R White (undated) *Young People, Crime and Public Perceptions: A Review of the Literature* (Slough: National Foundation for Educational Research)

Hamilton, C (2005) *At the Police Station: The Role of the 'Appropriate Adult'*, Legal Guide (Colchester: Children's Legal Centre)

Hammersley, R, L Marsland and M Reid (2003) *Substance Use by Young Offenders: The Impact of the Normalization of Drug Use in the Early Years of the 21st Century,* Home Office Research Study 261 (London: Home Office Research and Statistics Directorate)

Hart, D (2014) *What's in a Name? The Identification of Children in Trouble with the Law* (London: Standing Committee for Youth Justice)

HM Chief Inspector of Prisons (2013) *Report on an Unannounced Inspection of HMP/YOI Feltham (Feltham A – Children and Young People) 21–25 January 2013* (London: Her Majesty's Inspectorate of Prisons)

HM Court Service/Youth Justice Board (2010) *Making it Count in Court* www.yjb.gov.uk/publications/Resources/Downloads/Making%20it%20count%20in%20court.pdf

HM Inspectorate of Constabulary with HM Inspectorate of Prisons, HM Inspectorate of Probation, Care Quality Commission, Healthcare Inspectorate Wales and Care and Social Services Inspectorate Wales (2011) *Who's Looking Out for the Children? A Joint Inspection of Appropriate Adult*

Provision and Children in Detention after Charge www.justice.gov.uk/downloads/publications/inspectorate-reports/hmipris/thematic-reports-and-research-publications/whos-looking-after-children.pdf

HM Inspectorate of Prisons (2003) *Juveniles in Custody: A Unique Insight into the Perceptions of Young People Held in Prison Service Custody in England and Wales* (London: HM Inspectorate of Prisons)

HM Inspectorate of Probation, HM Inspectorate of Courts Administration, HM Crown Prosecution Service Inspectorate (2011) *Not Making Enough Difference: A Joint Inspection of Youth Offending Court Work and Reports* www.justice.gov.uk/downloads/publications/inspectorate-reports/hmiprobation/Court_Work_and_Reports_Thematic_Report-rps.pdf

Home Office (2003) *Youth Justice: The Next Steps – Companion Document to Every Child Matters* (London: Home Office)

Home Office and Lord Chancellor's Department (2001) *The Youth Court 2001: The Changing Culture of the Youth Court – Good Practice Guide* (London: Home Office)

Hough, M and J V Roberts (2004) *Youth Crime and Youth Justice: Public Opinion in England and Wales* (Bristol: Policy Press)

House of Commons Home Affairs Committee (2007) *Young Black People and the Criminal Justice System*, HC 181-I (London: The Stationery Office)

Howard League for Penal Reform (1998) *Sentenced to Fail: Out of Sight, Out of Mind* (London: Howard League)

Howard League for Penal Reform (2009) *Analysis of the Inspectorate of Prisons Reports on Young Offender Institutions Holding Children in Custody* (London: Howard League)

Howard League for Penal Reform (2010) *Children and Long Sentences: A Briefing* (London: Howard League)

Howard League for Penal Reform (2012) *Resettlement: The Legal Rights of Children and Young People in the Criminal Justice System in Need of Accommodation and Support* (London: Howard League)

Howard League for Penal Reform (2013) *Overnight Detention of Children in Police Custody 2010–2011*, Research Briefing (London: Howard League)

Howard League for Penal Reform (2014) *U R Boss: Young People's Manifesto on Work and Education* www.urboss.org.uk/young-peoples-manifesto/work-and-education/education-campaign-2014

Howe, D (1996) 'Surface and depth in social work' in N Parton (ed.), *Social Theory, Social Change and Social Work* (London: Routledge)

Hucklesby, A (2013) 'The prosecution process' in A Hucklesby and A Wahidin (eds), *Criminal Justice* 2nd edn (Oxford: Oxford University Press) 83–104

Hucklesby, A and A Wahidin (2013) 'Introduction', in A Hucklesby and A Wahidin (eds), *Criminal Justice* 2nd edn (Oxford: Oxford University Press) 1–16

Hudson, S (2013) 'Because you're worth it: payment by results' 69(3) *Magistrate* 2–3

Independent Parliamentarians' Inquiry (2014) *Independent Parliamentarians' Inquiry into the Operation and Effectiveness of the Youth Court* www.ncb. org.uk/media/1148432/independent_parliamentarians__inquiry_into_ the_operation_and_effectiveness_of_the_youth_court.pdf
Inquest (2012) *Fatally Flawed* (London: Prison Reform Trust)
Inquest (2013) *List of Child Deaths in Penal Custody since 1990* (London: Inquest) www.inquest.org.uk/pdf/Deaths_of_Children_in_Penal_Custody_ 1990-date.pdf
Ipsos MORI (2006) *Attitudes Towards Teenagers and Crime* (London: Ipsos MORI) www.ipsos-mori.com/polls/2006/dispatches.shtml

Jenks, C (1996) *Childhood* (London: Routledge)
Johns, R (2011) *Using the Law in Social Work* 5th edn (Exeter: Learning Matters)
Johnstone, G and D W Van Ness (eds) (2007) *Handbook of Restorative Justice* (Cullompton: Willan)
Junger-Tas, J, G-J Terlouw and M W Klein (1994) *Delinquent Behaviour among Young People in the Western World: First Results on the International Self-report Delinquency Study* (Amsterdam: Kugler)
Justice.gov (2013) *Minimising and Managing Physical Restraint* www. justice.gov.uk/youth-justice/custody/behaviour-management/behaviour-management-and-restraint-update

Khan, L (2010) *Reaching Out, Reaching In: Promoting Mental Health and Emotional Well-being in Secure Settings* (London: Centre for Mental Health)
King, R D and R Morgan (1976) *A Taste of Prison: Custodial Conditions for Trial and Remand Prisoners* (London: Routledge & Kegan)

Lader, D, N Singleton and H Meltzer (2000) *Psychiatric Morbidity among Young Offenders in England and Wales* (London: Office for National Statistics)
Law Society (2012) *Response of the Law Society of England and Wales to 'Swift and Sure Justice: The Government's Plans for Reform of the Criminal Justice System'* www.lawsociety.org.uk/representation/policy-discussion/swift-and-sure-criminal-justice-system-reform-proposals/
Lipscombe, J (2006) *Care or Control? Foster Care for Young People on Remand* (London: British Association for Adoption and Fostering)
Lloyd C, I Wollny, C White, S Gowland and S Purdon (2011) *Monitoring and Evaluation of Family Intervention Services and Projects between February*

2007 and March 2011, Research Report DFE-RR174 (London: Department for Education)

Marlow, A (2005) 'The policing of young people', in T Bateman and J Pitts (eds), *The RHP Companion to Youth Justice* (Lyme Regis: Russell House)

McAra, L and S McVie (2010) 'Youth crime and justice: key messages from the Edinburgh study of youth transitions and crime' 10 *Criminology and Criminal Justice* 211–30

McConnochie, A (2009) *Preparing for the Scaled Approach: Learning from the Pilot – Information for Youth Offending Teams* (London: Youth Justice Board)

Medina Ariza, J J (2014). 'Police-initiated contacts: young people, ethnicity, and the "usual suspects"' 24(2) *Policing and Society: An International Journal of Research and Policy* 208–23

Ministry of Justice (undated) *Criminal Procedure Rules* www.justice.gov. uk/courts/procedure-rules/criminal

Ministry of Justice (2010) *Breaking the Cycle: Effective Punishment, Rehabilitation and Sentencing of Offenders,* Cm 7972 (London: The Stationery Office)

Ministry of Justice (2011) *Achieving Best Evidence in Criminal Proceedings* (London: The Stationery Office) www.justice.gov.uk/downloads/victims-and-witnesses/vulnerable-witnesses/achieving-best-evidence-criminal-proceedings.pdf

Ministry of Justice (2012) *Swift and Sure Justice: The Government's Plans for Reform of the Criminal Justice System*, Cm 8388 (London: The Stationery Office)

Ministry of Justice (2013a) *Statistics: Youth Custody Data* (London: Ministry of Justice) www.gov.uk/government/publications/youth-custody-data

Ministry of Justice (2013b) *Triennial Review of the Youth Justice Board for England and Wales: Combined Report on Stages One and Two* (London: Ministry of Justice) https://consult.justice.gov.uk/digital-communications/yjb-triennial-review-2012/results/triennial-review-yjb-stages1–2.pdf

Ministry of Justice (2013c) *Transforming Management of Young Adults in Custody*, Cm 8733 (London: The Stationery Office)

Ministry of Justice (2014) *Youth Custody Report: January 2014* (London: Ministry of Justice)

Ministry of Justice/National Offender Management Service (2012) *The Transition Process: Guidance on Transfers from Under 18 Young Offender Institutions to Young Adult Young Offender Institutions* (London: MoJ) www.justice.gov.uk/youth-justice/youth-to-adult-transitions/guidance-on-transfers-from-under-18-young-offender-institutions-to-young-adult-young-offender-institutions

Ministry of Justice/National Offender Management Service/Multi-Agency Public Protection Arrangements (2012) *MAPPA Guidance 2012*, Version 4

(London: National MAPPA Team/National Offender Management Service/Offender Management and Public Protection Group)

Ministry of Justice/Youth Justice Board (undated/a) *Injunctions to Prevent Gang-Related Violence: Supporting Documentation for Youth Offending Teams* www.justice.gov.uk/youth-justice/courts-and-orders/disposals/gang-injunctions

Ministry of Justice/Youth Justice Board (undated/b) *Youth Out-of-Court Disposals: Guide for Police and Youth Offending Services* www.justice.gov.uk/downloads/youth-justice/courts-and-orders/laspo/out-court-disposal-guide.pdf

Ministry of Justice/Youth Justice Board (2012) *Referral Order Guidance* (London: Ministry of Justice)

Ministry of Justice/Youth Justice Board (2014) *Youth Justice Statistics 2012//13 England and Wales* (London: Ministry of Justice/Youth Justice Board)

Moore, S A and R C Mitchell (2009) 'Rights-based restorative justice: evaluating compliance with international standards' 9(1) *Youth Justice* 27–43

Muncie, J and G Hughes (2002) 'Modes of youth governance: political rationalities, criminalization and resistance' in J Muncie, G Hughes and E McLaughlin (eds), *Youth Justice: Critical Readings* (London: Sage) 1–18

Munro, E (2011) *Munro Review of Child Protection: Final Report – A Child Centred System* (London: Department for Education)

NACRO (1998) *Briefing: Bail Support* (London: NACRO)

NACRO (2002) *Children who Commit Grave Crimes* (London: NACRO)

NACRO (2008) *Children's Human Rights and the Youth Justice System*, Youth Crime Briefing (London: NACRO)

National Policing Improvement Agency (2012) *Guidance on the Safer Detention and Handling of Persons in Police Custody* 2nd edn (Hook: National Policing Improvement Agency, published on behalf of the Association of Chief Police Officers)

Newburn, T (2013) *Criminology* 2nd edn (Oxford: Routledge)

Nuffield Foundation (2011) *Impact of Special Measures on Jury Decision-making* www.nuffieldfoundation.org/impact-special-measures-jury-decision-making

O'Mahoney, P (2009) 'The risk factors prevention paradigm and the cause of youth crime: a deceptively useful analysis?' 9(2) *Youth Justice* 99–114

Paylor, I (2010) 'The scaled approach to youth justice: a risky business' September *Criminal Justice Matters*

Pickford, J (2000) *Youth Justice: Theory and Practice* (London: Cavendish)

Pickford, J and P Dugmore (2012) *Youth Justice and Social Work* 2nd edn (London: Sage Learning Matters)

Pierpont, H (2004) 'A survey of volunteer appropriate adult services in England and Wales' 4(1) *Youth Justice* 32–45

Prison Reform Trust (2009) *Vulnerable Defendants in the Criminal Courts: A Review of Provision for Adults and Children* (London: Prison Reform Trust)

Prison Reform Trust (2010) *Seen and Heard: Supporting Vulnerable Children in the Youth Justice System* (London: Prison Reform Trust)

Prison Reform Trust (2011) *Care: A Stepping Stone to Custody?* (London: Prison Reform Trust)

Prison Reform Trust (2012) *Fair Access to Justice? Support for Vulnerable Defendants in the Criminal Courts* (London: Prison Reform Trust)

Prison Reform Trust and Young Minds (2013) *Turning Young Lives Around* (London: Prison Reform Trust)

Reiner, R (1985) *The Politics of the Police* (Brighton: Wheatsheaf)

Ross, A, K Duckworth, D J Smith, G Wyness and I Schoon (2011) *Prevention and Reduction: A Review of Strategies for Intervening Early to Prevent or Reduce Youth Crime and Anti-social Behaviour*, Research Report DFE-RR111 Centre for Analysis of Youth Transitions/Department for Education (London: Institute for Fiscal Studies)

Rutter, M, H Giller and A Hagell (1998) *Antisocial Behaviour by Young People* (Cambridge: Cambridge University Press)

Sentencing Council (2011) *Overarching Guidelines Consultation: Allocation, Offences Taken into Consideration and Totality* (London: Sentencing Council)

Sentencing Guidelines Council (2009) *Overarching Principles: Sentencing Youth – Definitive Guide* (London: Sentencing Guidelines Council)

Shapland, J, A Atkinson, H Atkinson, E Colledge, J Dignan, M Howes, J Johnstone, G Robinson and A Sorsby (2006) 'Situating restorative justice within criminal justice' 10(4) *Theoretical Criminology* 505–32

Smith, R (2007) *Youth Justice: Ideas, Policy, Practice* (Cullompton: Willan)

Souhami, A (2008) 'Multi-agency practice: experiences in the youth justice system' in S Green, E Lancaster and S Feasey (eds), *Addressing Offending Behaviour: Context, Practice and Values* (Cullompton: Willan) 208–25

Souhami, A (2013) 'Youth justice' in A Hucklesby and A Wahidin (eds), *Criminal Justice* 2nd edn (Oxford: Oxford University Press) 222–46

Staines, J (2013) 'The implementation of restorative approaches in a secure child care centre' 1(3) *Restorative Justice: An International Journal* 362–88

Stone, N (2010a) 'Legal commentary: developments in determining mode of trial for grave allegations' 10(1) *Youth Justice* 73–83

Stone, N (2010b) 'Legal commentary: special measures for child defendants – a decade of developments' 10(2) *Youth Justice* 174–85

Stone, N (2012) 'Legal commentary: juveniles with adult co-accused – venue for trial and sentence' 12(1) *Youth Justice* 53–63

Strickland, P (2013) *The Abolition of Sentences of Imprisonment for Public Protection*, Commons Library Standard Note Sn06086 (London: House of Commons Library) www.parliament.uk/briefing-papers/Sn06086

Sutherland, E (1947) *Principles of Criminology* 4th edn (Philadelphia: J B Lippincott)

Talbot, J (2012) 'Fair access to justice?' 68(8) *Magistrate* 6

Thomas, S (2005) *National Evaluation of the Bail Supervision and Support Schemes Funded by the Youth Justice Board for England and Wales from April 1999 to March 2002* (London: Youth Justice Board)

UN Committee on the Rights of the Child (2007) *General Comment No 10: Children's Rights in Juvenile Justice*, CRC/C/GC/10 (Geneva: UN) www2. ohchr.org/english/bodies/crc/docs/CRC.C.GC.10.pdf

UN Committee on the Rights of the Child (2008) *Consideration of Reports Submitted by States Parties under Article 44 of the Convention – Concluding Observations*, CRC/C/GBR/CO/4 (Geneva: UN) www2.ohchr.org/english/ bodies/crc/docs/AdvanceVersions/CRC.C.GBR.CO.4.pdf

Wain, N with E Burney (2007) *The ASBO: Wrong Turning, Dead End* (London: Howard League)

Waiton, S (2001) *Scared of the Kids? Curfews, Crime and the Regulation of Young People* (Sheffield: Sheffield Hallam University)

Walgrave, L (2000) 'How pure can a maximalist approach to restorative justice remain? Or can a purist model of restorative justice become maximalist? 3(4) *Contemporary Justice Review* 415–32

Walker, J, C Thompson, G Wilson and K Laing with M Coombes and S Raybould (2008) *Family Group Conferencing in Youth Inclusion and Support Panels: Empowering Families and Preventing Crime and Antisocial Behaviour?* (London: Youth Justice Board)

Winfield, M (1984) *Lacking Conviction: The Remand System in England and Wales* (London: Prison Reform Trust)

Youth Justice Board (2005) *Role of Risk and Protective Factors* (London: Youth Justice Board)

Youth Justice Board (2008a) *Assessment, Intervention Planning and Supervision* (London: Youth Justice Board)

Youth Justice Board (2008b) *Evaluation of the Youth Inclusion Programme* (London: Youth Justice Board)

Youth Justice Board (2010a) *A Report on the Intensive Fostering Pilot Programme* (London: Youth Justice Board)

Youth Justice Board (2010b) *The Youth Rehabilitation Order and Other Youth Justice Provisions of the Criminal Justice and Immigration Act 2008 (B422): Practice Guidance for Youth Offending Teams* (London: Youth Justice Board)

Youth Justice Board (2011) *Youth Restorative Disposal Process Evaluation* (London: Youth Justice Board)

Youth Justice Board (2013a) *National Standards for Youth Justice Services* (London: Youth Justice Board)

Youth Justice Board (2013b) *Assessment and Planning Interventions Framework*, AssetPlus National YOT and Secure Establishment Briefing (June) (London: Youth Justice Board)

Youth Justice Board (2013c) *Care Planning for Young People on Remand in England and Wales* (London: Youth Justice Board)

INDEX